Ten Years Behind

THE

Sacred Desk

by

FLOYD N. BRADLEY

ISBN 0-88019-232-1

Schmul Publishing Co., Inc.
Wesleyan Book Club   Salem, Ohio
1988

DEDICATION

Lovingly dedicated to my devoted wife who has so faithfully stood by me in every conflict and so willingly shared in every joy and sorrow.

CONTENTS

INTRODUCTION

I read a book sometime ago giving an incident of a gentleman introducing a young minister to an eminent juror. The judge responded, "I hope he preaches the gospel in its simplicity." The common people are attracted to the simple teaching of the gospel. They do not want it ornamented with flowers of rhetoric or presented in a language that would require an interpreter as do the missionaries in foreign lands.

This autobiography is so simple and clear in its statements that any child can understand it. It is full of graphic, lifesize pictures. It will inspire any reader. Usually you find the first chapter of a book the most interesting, but when you have once started this one you will have difficulty in finding a place where you want to stop. The farther you read the more you read the more fascinating it becomes. You are held with the wonder of what is coming next.

This book will be a blessing to young Christians who feel a call into some religious work and have no open doors. It will help those who are having trouble with false teachings, fanaticism, and wild fire. After reading the book you will never be the same. I have never read of greater tests of faith, trials of patience, persecutions, answers to prayer or victories won. In fact I have never read of so many things to try the faith of God's children happening in such a short period of time.

Do not fail to read this book. And may the Holy Ghost bless you abundantly.

John T. Hatfield

PREFACE

Our aim in the writing of this book has not been to exalt self or uphold any personal accomplishments, but rather to exalt Christ and give forth some facts, proving that the God of Elijah is the same today, "the Living God that changes not." Be it known to all that we laid our sinful self at the feet of the Saviour and for whatever has been done, to Him be all of the glory.

> "Nothing in my hands I bring,
> Simply to Thy cross I cling,
> Naked, come to Thee for dress,
> Helpless, come to Thee for grace."

The suggestion to put our experience into print was first made by our dear father. After giving it prayerful consideration we felt that it would be pleasing to God.

Whatever is contained within the covers of this book has been written with prayerful heart and believing that God would use it for His glory: perhaps to help some that feel the call to the great harvest field, perhaps a young preacher on the verge of discouragement, or some of the more mature saints that need a stimulant for their faith in the face of some fiery trial through which they may be passing.

During our ten years of work for the Master we have had a combination of joys and sorrows, prosperities and adversities, hard places and easy ones, but the grace of God has been our sufficiency. We have never been sorry that we answered the call and, if we had a thousand lives to live, we would give them all to Jesus.

Someone has said, "May there be enough clouds in the sky of your life to make a beautiful sunset." This is our heart's desire, to be crushed and moulded and fashioned in the hand of the Master. We have seen many that were on fire for God in their early ministry, according to all reports, while today finds them prayerless, lifeless, juiceless and joyless; some are spiritual wrecks on the shores of time. May God help us to keep red-hot, much in prayer and growing in grace. If we felt that we would cool off, we would want to go home to Glory now while we are in the midst of the battle with precious Blood-bought victory in our soul.

We have found in our short experience that every cloud has a silver lining and that every blow can be a boost. Whether joys or sorrows are before us, we know not; but we welcome the will of God whatever it may bring.

It is the prayer of our heart, that if Jesus tarries and we live to an old age, that it will not find us sour and critical, but as sweet as Heaven and as fragrant as the Rose of Sharon. When the sun of life has kissed the western horizon of time, and the boatman is waiting to convey us across the river of death to the shores of fair deliverance, whether young or old, we want to be found "dressed in His righteousness alone, faultless to stand before His Throne."

All for Jesus,

FLOYD N. BRADLEY.

CHAPTER I

CONVERSION AND CALL

It was a hazy afternoon the last of September, but in spite of the shadows there was a peculiar illumination in my heart and a glimmer of hope in my mind that seemed to turn clouds into sunshine. Was it possible? I seemed to ask myself the question, as the trolley sped along through the country. Here were my bags; in my pockets was a hundred dollars toward my tuition, and I was on my way to the little town of Pennington where the school was located. I confess I wasn't very much interested in the scenery, though it was beautiful, for my mind was building the most wonderful air castles. What evangelist would I be traveling with five years from this afternoon? Would it be in some great tabernacle campaign with some world-famed preacher? Just what did the future hold for me? Would I make a success? The bit of ego that I had led me to believe that I could surely be an accomplished song leader in a short time.

What was that? Pennington! Yes, the conductor had called it. I suddenly came to earth and realized that I was at my destination. I wasn't long grabbing my luggage and getting off the car. I went up to the school, met Dr. G——, and registered. It wasn't long until I was in the room assigned to me, and was arranging my things and unpacking my clothes. There,

9

it was finished; everything in order, and this was to
be my home for at least nine months, providing I
could raise the balance of my tuition.

It surely was wonderful how God had led. I must
give you a brief sketch of my conversion and call to
this sacred work which I so much enjoy. It has been
far different from what I pictured, and with a combination of joys and sorrows, appointments and dis-
appointments, I have attained to my present Christian
experience.

I can truly say with the poet, " 'Tis grace that
brought me safe thus far, and grace will lead me
home."

I was just sixteen years old. My father had bought
me a suit of long trousers for the occasion, and my
birthday fell on Sunday. Surely I was a man now.
I strutted down the street to the church that we attended hoping that every one would notice my new at-
tire. I had been going to the services nearly every
night for two weeks and now the last Sunday had
arrived, but the last Sunday of a series of meetings
meant nothing to me in those days. If I remember
correctly, the church was well filled, it seated perhaps
eight hundred on the main floor. The evangelist, Dr.
Bromley, of Wilmore, Kentucky, preached a faithful
message and at the inivation I stood with the rest of
the Christians. Was I a Christian? Why certainly!
I had joined the church when I was twelve and later
was taken in as a full member. Folks cried when we
joined and of course we cried too, and that's as much
as I remember about it. However foreign that was to
conversion, it did play an important part in restrain-

ing us and holding us in the church. There was one
other reason why I certainly was a Christian. It was
that they had given me a Sunday School class of small
boys, and also an office in the Epworth League. How
could any one doubt that I was a Christian?

In the evening I returned to the closing service with
a young man who was also a teacher in the Sunday
School. I was of course interested in the success of
the meetings, but not from the standpoint of snatch-
ing souls as brands from the burning. If I remember
there had been quite a few forward and bowed
at the altar in the old-fashioned style.

The preliminaries were over, and Dr. Bromley was
taking his place behind the sacred desk. I do not remember his text; I do not remember his sermon nor
one illustration that he gave. I surely was listening,
for I was always attentive in the services. The only
thing that I do remember was that I did not feel just
right. In spite of the fact that I was a member of
the church, I confess I did not feel ready for Heaven.
Heretofore my theology was that you were ready for
Heaven if you belonged to the church, and especially
the Methodist Church. I must say that when the
Spirit began dealing with me that Sunday night, February 21, 1920, He changed my theological views in a
very few minutes. The sermon was ended, the invitation hymn was given and the congregation asked to
rise. I arose with the rest and gripped the back of the
seat. There I stood halting between two opinions;
surely this was the valley of decision for me. I realized my need, it seemed that the sins of my childhood
were mountain high and that I was on the brink of

eternity. What an anguish of soul, what a state of mind! The fight was on. The devil pointed out the various people that had confidence in me, and there were some of the boys from my class, and their parents. How could I go? What would they think? The more I thought of it the tighter I gripped the pew. One or two had gone, but how could I get grace enough to step out? The aisle seemed twice as long as it was and the devil had everything magnified. The hymn ended and for the benefit of those that had not made a start as yet, they sang "Almost Persuaded." Praise God for His mercy in directing them to hold on a little longer. What if they had not? I might have been writhing in the pit of perdition and remembering throughout the endless ages of eternity that altar call, and that service.

They were on the last stanza, oh, what a struggle! I never shall forget it. Finally with my heart pounding like a trip-hammer, and with a lump in my throat, I left my seat and hurried down the aisle and fell at the altar. I had hardly struck the altar when the tears began to flow like rain; my heart was broken and contrite. How I prayed and wept and confessed! And after a real siege in the old-fashioned way the victory came. Praise God, it was certainly different from the time I joined the church.

What joy, what peace, what brightness! They talk about feeling, well I had about all I could take care of. When I looked up everything seemed different; things had taken on a new aspect, and I had suddenly been born from above and adopted into the family of God. Why shouldn't I feel differently? I went there a

pauper and arose in possession of the wealth of
Heaven. I fell on my face a child of the devil and got
on my feet a child of the King. Amen!

How much more there is to salvation than just getting it. How necessary that we walk in the light and
be obedient to the heavenly vision in order to retain a
relationship to God. Paul stresses it by saying, "Work
out your own salvation with fear and trembling."
The Lord help every reader not to do as Lot's wife,
go so far and then look back, but rather to keep pressing toward the mark of the prize of the high calling
of God.

I was sure that God had saved me. I knew my sins
were gone, I felt so clean and bright. It did seem as
though I were living in a new world. I had forgotten
all about the time; I had been facing eternity. It was
already after eleven o'clock when we left the church,
and father and mother were quite strict about our
being in early; so we hurried on. Thank God for a
father and mother, though not enjoying a Christian
experience, who were careful to keep my brother and
me under their control. Well, I was sure they would
understand since my aunt and her friend were with
me, and then, too, I thought they might be in bed. We
hurried and finally reached my home. As I went up
the steps I saw father was standing by the window.
I knew I had a legitimate excuse, and so prepared to
give it; however, I was glad that my aunt went in
with me. When I got into the room father wanted to
know where I had been until such an hour. I said,
"I've been to church." "Now don't try to tell me that,"
he said, "no church keeps in this late." Well, I don't

know that I could blame him for such a statement; it
was very rare, and I suppose he wasn't expecting the
unusual. It must have stirred him to think I would
lie to him and so, before my aunt could explain, I had
a couple of hard slaps on the side of the jaw and was
told to go to bed. Well, I didn't stay to plead my
case but ascended the stairs as fast as I could. There
were a few harsh words below, the slam of the door,
and father was on his way to bed.

Thank God, real Bible salvation will stand to be
misunderstood, and when the possessor is slapped, instead of knocking it out, it just knocks it further in.
Amen! I went to bed determined to live for God.
That slap, and from one who felt justified, drove me
up the road. Someone has said, "Blows hurt, but they
help." It is the hard blows from the sculptor's ham-
mer and chisel that bring out the beauties of the
statue.

I began to attend the prayer meeting regularly and
to testify and pray. I saw the wrong of the moving
pictures and ceased going. Besides I had many other
convictions. As I look back I can see how I was growing. If only I could have had some real spiritual person to take an interest in me and show me the privilege and possibility of being sanctified. However,
God's hand was in it all, so we say Amen to His will.
I continued to grow well from the time of my conversion in February until about the last of May when, at
one of our Sunday evening services in the church
where I was converted, there was a returned missionary with costumes and curios from the field. He
gave a stirring message and told of the need of Chris-

tian workers. As he talked I felt the Lord dealing with my heart and calling me into His service. At the close of the meeting I walked home with the same aunt and friend, mentioned above. I told them what I felt, but they seemed to think it was just a desire. The young man talked to me quite a little and told what it meant—the hardships of a servant of God whose life was dedicated to the work and, then, what an awful thing to go if it was not really of God. I took it all in but made up my mind I would do as I felt, regardless of other people's opinions. Just before this I had left school in my third year of high school and had gone to work on the railroad. I did not like school any too well; it seemed as though I would study and study and could not learn. I enjoyed working. I was making pretty good money for a boy and I had said, "No more school for me."

After a few weeks continually feeling the call of the Lord and not knowing just how to go about the thing, I determined to talk it over with someone who would be in sympathy with me. I knew of none better to go to than my pastor.

One hot afternoon in July I stopped to see him. I told him how I felt, what prompted my feeling and how it had lingered with me. He seemed very sympathetic and glad and, being a highly educated man, naturally laid out the same plan which he had pursued. "Now first," (I can almost hear him say it now) "Floyd, you better go back to high school in the fall and finish your course." What an awful blow to a fellow who had made such a rash decision, and who seemed as thick-headed as I! Then he went on, "I would suggest four years' college" (naming a certain institution), "then you will be ready for your three-year theological course at such a seminary." "Well, but isn't there any other way, Mr. V——?" "No, Floyd, you must have such an education as I have described in order to qualify for a church in almost all of the denominations." Well, while he was talking, I was figuring. It would be eight years before I could preach. I felt as though I was about ready then; surely, I knew the books of the Bible in order and a few Bible characters. What would hinder me from qualifying?

I must confess I left the parsonage discouraged. I could not learn like others; I hated school anyway, and I never would go back. That was settled. Well, I not only settled the school question and with it the preaching question, but also the question of any further growth in my experience. That school proposition was like a mountain. The devil used that to break my determination to go with God. Oh, I did not intend to give up my experience, but I just would not go to school.

Sad it is, many folks do not intend to lose out and backslide, but when they refuse to go on, there is no other way but back. "If we walk in the light, as he is in the light, we have fellowship one with another, and the blood of Jesus Christ his Son cleanseth us from all sin." As I reflect on the past, I see how from the very afternoon, just mentioned, I began losing the precious experience that I had so much enjoyed. I believe, from observation, that my own experience is a picture of many souls that run well for a season and then because of some big thing or little thing they rebel against light.

I began losing ground, but it was so slowly, and the enemy of my soul was so subtle, that I did not detect the downward grade. How cunning old Satan is! How many, like myself, he has led astray and, in the time of an emergency, how they would spring to their feet, shake themselves as before and, like Samson, "knew not that the Lord had departed from them." It was not long until I ventured into the moving picture show and it did not seem so bad; I rather enjoyed it. I do not believe that it was more than three months from that time until I was spending the greater part of my spare time in the theatre.

In the meantime, I had received a promotion from the baggage department to the passenger ticket department with an increase in salary. In this position I came in contact with men and women that were old in the sin business. What a trap for a sixteen-year-old boy. Thank God for His mercy to me! No one knew the battles that I fought alone, the contact with sin of the lower type, the vulgar talk, the smutty stories, the making light of things that are sacred. I did not realize it then as I do now that I look back. I did not see that slowly I was absorbing the influences that were around me, and all of this without God. Oh, yes, I had a profession; I still attended church when I did not have to work, but the world was getting me in its net. Sin was getting its grip upon my heart. I began smoking and entering into some of the conversations that were far from edifying.

God help the young people of today! God have mercy on the older people who are acting as agencies in the hands of Satan to teach the younger generation the ways of sin and vice! Would to God I had never seen some of them. But, thank God, the past is all under the blood and my heart rejoices for redemption full and free.

I was working odd hours, sometimes until midnight and then I would go home with some of the folks until early morning. Father and mother would question me, but I had to work overtime. They did not know all; I suppose they believed what I said. God bless them, they did their best from a material and moral standpoint. It is like a nightmare as I recall those days; it was pleasure while it was on, but oh, the aftermath.

Finally I became acquainted with a young woman who was very worldly. but who was beautiful and subtle. I was attracted and began keeping company with her. I had just passed my seventeenth birthday; she was perhaps a year or two my senior, and very winning in her way.

During this period there were times when I would resolve to do different. I would talk with her. I would get down to pray before I left and oh, what a time of praying and crying! She would look at me as though I had lost my mind. I would stand waiting for a street car late at night; perhaps I had been playing my violin at a dance, or coming from the home of the above-mentioned girl; how I would make new resolutions, but only to break them in a day or two.

With all my lying, with all of my deceitfulness with my parents, with all my hypocrisy in the church, with all of the degrading influence of a railroad ticket office and all of the chance to plunge to the very depth of sin, God, bless His name, had His hand upon me and kept me from immorality. Why shouldn't I praise Him? No one but Divinity and the demons of the pit knew just how near the slimy edge of the precipice of sin I was, and yet at the same time I was a member of the church, and an officer in the young people's organization. Thank God, that "where sin abounds grace doth much more abound."

In the midst of this awful tangle of sin, the Lord began talking to my heart. I began writing to different schools about taking work, but it seemed that nothing developed; the way was blocked.

In the early summer of 1921, one balmy night I went home from the office with more concern than usual about my soul's salvation. It was late; the folks were in bed and so I retired. Brother was away and I was sleeping alone. This night, instead of tumbling into bed and going to sleep as usual, I lay awake quite awhile. In the quietude of that hot summer night God began to speak to me. He showed me the past year and a half since my conversion, my refusal to go to school and prepare myself for His work, the slow but sure grip that sin was getting upon my heart, and the awfulness of eternity without His mercy. Then came the same old question, "Will you preach? Will you give me your life for service, regardless of how many years of preparation it may mean?" By the time the Spirit brought me to that question, I was weeping bitterly; the hot tears were scalding my cheeks while I rolled and tossed on my bed. When the question came I was ready to say, "Yes." My stubborn will was yielded and oh, what a Divine illumination filled my soul! Praise God and the Lamb forever! Who was I that He should deal with me so faithfully!

> "Grace, grace, God's grace,
> Grace that will pardon and cleanse within,
> Grace, grace, God's grace,
> Grace that is greater than all our sin."

It seemed that night that I fell asleep on the bosom of Jesus. Thank God for the times since when, in deep despair and anguish of heart, I have found rest and consolation in Him.

I began immediately to check up on my prayer life and also my conduct; I was not very stable as I would see it now, but I was at least doing all I could to make the grade. I took more of an interest in the work of the church and did my best to attend the prayer meetings when possible.

It was not long until a young people's institute was to be held at Pennington Seminary, near Trenton, New Jersey. It was to last for a week and delegates from the Methodist Church were to attend. I was asked to take charge of the singing and so, wanting to be prominent, I accepted the offer and prepared to go.

I was there for the opening service, dressed up like a peacock and feeling keenly myself important. The singing went over big, and surely Floyd N. B—— felt bigger. Though full of pride, I see that God was leading me away from the lure of the world to realize that the things of eternity are those of real worth. In the classes during the day and also during the preaching service I realized as never before the seriousness of the Divine call.

At the close of the week I was called to the office of the head-master of the seminary who was on the grounds and in many of the services. I had publicly dedicated my life for full time Christian service and some knew that I wanted, or rather needed, some training. He told me the good points about the school and told me I could finish my high school subjects as well as take some Bible work. He gave me the privilege of leading the singing in chapel services and said he would allow me $100.00 on my tuition. This was fine. I reached at the opportunity and told him I would be there for the opening, the last of September.

I met with some opposition at home; was told that the ministry was a beggar's profession, along with other encouraging remarks. Beggar's profession or not, I was set like a flint and carried out my purpose.

CHAPTER II

A MAKESHIFT PREACHER

Well, I almost felt like a preacher, but the question was how would I feel when I went into the pulpit. I comforted myself with the thought that I had had enough part in public meetings that I at least could keep myself composed. I continued scanning my notes and rehearsing over and over what I intended to say. I had chosen the thirteenth chapter of 1 Corinthians as my lesson and the basis of the sermon, if it could be called such, and had read Henry Drummond's book through in order to be more apt in the exposition of the lesson. The nearer the trolley got to Marshall's Corner the more peculiar I felt. Do you ask why? Well, this was to be my first sermon. Oh, I had spoken a little in the young people's meetings at home, but this was to be a real church service with its organ prelude and postlude and the following of the regular Methodist ritual for the Sunday morning service. I am sure I did not look much like a preacher and I know that I did not feel much like one.

When I arrived I hastily made a general survey of the locality. It was a country place with about three houses and a blacksmith shop. I noticed a truck standing a few rods from the car stop, and in a minute a rather young man got out and approached me. I made up my mind that he was one of the official board and had come to meet me as prearranged. Well,

here was where the dignity proposition had to begin.
I at least had to act as I had seen the preachers act,
even though I did not look and feel like one. It was
a pretty hard job for me, being only a boy of seventeen years old, to act like some of the old starched
fellows that I had been used to seeing, but I made an
attempt whether for better or for worse I know not.
We were soon in the truck and on the road to the
church, it was not many minutes, for it was only four
or five miles, before we were at the Linvale Methodist
Church. It was a country church large enough for
perhaps a hundred and fifty people. The autos were
parked in quite thickly, with a few carriages here and
there. My what a feeling! The folks were all there,
apparently, to hear the new preacher and prospective
pastor, much depending on the kind of a sermon that
he preached.

Sunday School was about over and it was not long
until, when I was ascending the steps to the rostrum.
I dropped on my knees and with much the same feeling that one has when about to propose to his sweetheart, I breathed a humble prayer. At the appointed
time I arose and announced the first hymn and determined to brace up and put on a good front if I did
not have much in back. God did wonderfully sustain
me and gave me a calmness that was almost unbelievable to me; surely Divine help was mine in the
delivering of that first "makeshift sermon." In spite
of all the help that the Lord gave me I must confess
that I was plenty warm enough through the entire
service, in fact, I would have been far more comfortable that morning if there had been no fire in the

church. I had not been wearing glasses very long and was not altogether used to them. On this occasion I was so warm that my glasses became steamed over with the intense heat from my face and I found this quite embarrassing and made up my mind that they were more of a liability than an asset. Well, praise God for helping in these early experiences; without His help no doubt we would have gotten discouraged and given up.

At the close of the service I took my place at the door and most every one shook my hand cordially; I was introduced to a Mrs. D—— with whom I was to take dinner. I drove home with these dear folks and was escorted into the living room and introduced to the family. Of course, I was the very highly esteemed Reverend; I surely would have to put on my dignity now. One thing that bothered me greatly was a fear that someone would approach me on my age; whenever anyone would verge on this subject I would get very uneasy and do my best to change the course of the conversation. I felt that surely if they found out I was only seventeen they never would call me as their pastor. Well, finally the dinner was ready and so was I. What a dinner—chicken and everything! They surely would not set me down to such a typical preacher's meal if they did not think I was one.

The question arose as to the afternoon appointment. I knew there was one, but I had not thought of a second sermon for that occasion. I had only one and didn't know where I could find another between the dinner hour and the service for the afternoon appoint-

.ment. It was decided after awhile, and much to my comfort, that the father who had not been to the morning service would drive me over. I drew a sigh of relief and knew that I would be all set to use the same sermon.

We arrived at the little church back in the hills and rocks, mostly rocks. There were few present and this made the whole thing very personal. We had prayer and as is customary with the Methodists I felt obliged to close with the Lord's Prayer. This was not a cross for I had known it from childhood. But on this occasion, in the middle of it I completely forgot and, as there were such a few in the congregation, it was very noticeable. Surely the drops of perspiration rolled down my back. This disturbed me greatly and I had quite a job to get myself adjusted. I was glad when the service was over, and no doubt the people were too.

One day, the next week, I was called to the office to answer a telephone call. To my surprise it was Dr. S——, the district superintendent, "Well, Mr. B——," he said, "the folks at Linvale enjoyed the service Sunday and want you to serve them as pastor." Well what a shock! I do not remember what I said, it stunned me so. I went to my room. "Pastor of a church and only seventeen," I said to myself. I could hardly believe it. What could I preach to them? How could I find a different sermon for every Sunday? What would they do if they found out I was so young? A host of questions flooded my mind in rapid succession, to think that I had been in school only about six weeks, knew practically nothing

about the Bible except what I had learned in Sunday
School. Here were other boys much older and better
qualified than I. Well, I could not figure it out,
and the only way I can now is that "God works in a
mysterious way His wonders to perform". He was
surely working Romans 8:28 out in my life, "All
things work together for good to them that love God,
to them who are the called according to his purpose".
This was one of the "all things".

I had been preaching about six weeks and the Lord
had wonderfully unfolded the Word to me and had
given the message for each Sunday as the weeks
slipped by. They came so easy, and having preached
"*so long*" I felt like an "old timer", therefore I became somewhat lax in study. This week, I gave very
little time or thought to the services for Sunday, but
had a great deal of confidence in my ability and felt
sure that I could pick something up the last minute.
The last minute arrived, but I had no sermon. All
that I had was a text and it was not inspired to
my heart. All the way to the church I tried to call
to mind some thoughts that would be helpful in building that sermon, but my mind seemed blank.

I went into the pulpit; the time arrived for the
sermon. I arose and took my text, rambled and
took it again; talked all over myself and took it
again. I don't know how many times I took it
that service, but I know that every time I felt my
temperature rising. Finally, I sat down in disgrace;
I was whipped. I felt as if I could never preach
again. Thank God, that He took this early opportunity in my ministry to show me how futile our own

efforts are without His blessing upon them. I realized that if I did not study and store something in the warehouse of my mind there would be nothing for the Spirit to bring to my remembrance.

The next week I started on Monday to make preparation for Sunday. How I did dig in, and the Lord showed me that I should make a public confession to the congregation. This was a great deal for a fellow who still had in his possession the carnal mind. I finally consented and in the morning service I confessed to the congregation. I felt better immediately and had Divine help in the delivering of the message.

I had become very much interested in a young girl in T——, a few miles from the school. I had met her at the Young People's Institute the summer before and since I had been attending Seminary had visited her quite a little. I was feeling more and more interested and had begun to think that she would make a pretty good preacher's wife. I was seeing more and more that the girl with whom I had been going, back home, would make a very poor preacher's wife.

It was a tight place, for though I was not engaged to M——, back home, yet I had done some very serious talking; she had recently given me a $12.00 present which made the situation more grave. If ever a fellow prayed earnestly, I did. I laugh about it now, but I could not see a bit of humor in it then.

Well, the Lord surely answered prayer for the next letter I wrote received no answer. To give her every benefit of the doubt, I felt obliged to write again.

I did and still there was no answer.   My, I felt like a young colt that had been turned into the pasture.

It was nearly conference time and since I had never been to conference I at least wanted to go looking like a preacher.   I didn't have a black suit nor black shoes, so I decided to get both and wore them to church the Sunday before conference.

It was in March; it had begun to thaw and the roads were very muddy.   One of the men took me to the afternoon appointment.   It being a dirt road or rather a mud road we got stuck and I had to go afoot. I was all dressed up in my new suit and shoes and had no overshoes.   I had about three miles to go and every step I took I went deeper in the mire.   After a time trying to pick my way down the road I thought I would take to the field.   I did this but only to find that it was about as bad.   I was first on one side of the fence and then on the other, and that literally. My shoes were ruined, I thought, and as I climbed the fence to get back in the road—R-I-P—there!   I had torn my trousers of my brand new suit.   After a long gloomy jog in the mud, I reached the church full of my subject, "new shoes and suit ruined."   I found a few waiting, though the hour of service was past.   We had prayer together, they paid me the back salary and I started for the school.

After conference I decided that with such a circuit, I should have a little Ford to go in.   I was kept pretty busy during the week and Sunday was an exceptionally hard day.   I had to prepare my lessons, get my sermon, give six music lessons a week and press clothes for the boys on the side.   On Sunday

I had to preach twice and walk from six to ten miles, so I had little time left. However, I did go to T—— occasionally to see L——.

I found what I thought was a bargain in a Ford at $125.00. I had about $50.00, so I wrote to my brother and borrowed $75.00 and made the deal. It was for better or worse; I didn't have it long when I decided it was for worse. It took me there and brought me back, so I thought I would make the best of it. It had everything, even to rattles and flat tires; the front fenders were so well educated that they spoke to everyone on the road by flopping up and down. I had thought that my troubles would end, but instead they had just commenced.

It was beautiful spring weather and nearing the close of the school term. The air was balmy, the sun bright and the sky blue. Everything was conducive to having some nice young maid run off with one's heart. Well, that is just what happened and I was getting more and more convinced that a preacher should be married. Of course, all of these personal decisions were getting me near the "I will". We had a sort of mutual understanding and after exams were over and school was out L—— and I talked a little more seriously.

She had made application to go to Bible School in Chicago and I had felt a tug that way myself, so we decided that—well we were mutually agreed that we would settle it.

Yes, I was only eighteen, but I felt that I had found my mate for life and could we not get along better working together than separately? Her people did not object, but I knew mine would, seeing that I was so young. I did not know what to do. I thought, If I tell them and they object, then I will not want to go against their will; if I don't tell them, then I will have to face the music later.

The time was set and all the while L—— was trying to persuade me to tell my parents. I tried to get to it several times, but a lump in my throat seemed to prevail. It was the night before and still I had not told them. They knew that I was going with someone, and mother surmised that I was serious.

Without telling them, we were off to be married. Of course, we didn't need to hire a car with such a good little Ford as I owned, so we went in the Lizzy, noise and all. Naturally, we dressed in our very best and were in good spirits. On our way, my new straw hat blew off and down the street it went. This pricked my carnality some, and without thinking, I said, "Couldn't you catch that?" Poor Linda was broken-hearted to think that on our wedding day I would talk like that to her. Well I managed to get that patched up and we went on. We arrived at our destination, and then came the serious part.

The service was soon over, the knot was tied good and tight. Rev. A—— gave my wife the certificate and we left. When we got outside, wife said, "You didn't pay him." Oh, my, what a break! We went back and I humbly apologized while I pulled out a borrowed $10.00 bill and handed it to him. He, knowing that I was a preacher, folded the bill and handed it to Mrs. Bradley as a gift for herself. When we got in the car I was obliged to ask her for it so that I could pay it back to the one from whom I had borrowed it. Well, we were happy if we were poor. To think that the girl I had met eleven months before was my own bride.

After leaving the parsonage I noticed that Lizzy was boiling, so I drove up to a garage to get some water. It was a hot day and we had opened the wind-shield to get some air. I put the hose in the radiator and walked to the faucet, a few yards away, to turn on the water. When I did the tremendous force threw the hose out, squirting the water all over my bride. I grabbed for it and turned it on her again, and then all over myself. Well, what a calamity on our wedding day! Love is blind, for in a few minutes we had forgotten the spots all over our clothes.

We had been married about two weeks. Wife had been living with her aunt and I at my home thirty miles away. We saw each other over the week-end when I would go to my appointment. Life would be so happy if my parents only knew about it. I was not satisfied in keeping it from them, and my wife had never been; so we decided we would go and tell them. My wife came down, and Mother, Father, Linda and I went riding this Wednesday afternoon. We took a long ride and talked about everything, but I couldn't get courage to speak on the most important subject. Occasionally Linda would nod for me to tell them, but when I had it on my tongue I would get weak all over.

We got back home and when supper was ready, we sat down together. Well, there we sat; I would eat a bite or two and then look at my wife, and she would nod for me to go on. I would attempt it and lose my courage. What a time! Supper was over and I had not made any progress.

I said to my wife, "I think we had better go to prayer meeting". and I want to say that I surely did need such a meeting. She agreed and off we went to a Presbyterian Church for prayer service. It was a prayer meeting, for me, I don't know a thing that went on; I only know I was praying.

When service was out, Wife said, "Now, Dear, there is nothing else for us to do but go back and tell them". She was willing to tell them herself, but I wasn't. I wanted to do the telling—but.

We got home, went into the living room and there we sat. I swallowed, coughed, cleared my throat and then suddenly I would have a stoppage in my voice. The conversation went from one thing to another and then became strained. Things were tense. I saw that something had to be done so, after a great struggle, I said, "Well, we came to tell you that we are married." Father said, "You are married!" And Mother looked petrified. "Do you know that Floyd hasn't anything?" Father said. Wife replied, "We have Jesus, and that's all we need." We told them how long we had been married, and then there was another silence. Father arose from his chair and said, "Where are you staying?" "With my aunt", Wife replied. "Well, this is Floyd's home and since you are his wife it is your home. Bring your things here and feel free to call this your home."

What a wonderful attitude for an unsaved man! I was utterly whipped to think that Father, not being a Christian, would show such a beautiful spirit. Mother, too, was wonderful, but said, "I'm sorry because you are so young".

I have not been sorry of our union for I am satisfied that no wife would have been more willing to stand by me than my dear companion has been and is. Many times she has had only one dress to wear, night after night in revival meetings, one pair stockings which she would wash out at night and dry on the radiator, yet she did not complain but has helped me push the battle for God. Bless her dear heart!

I say it again, I have not been sorry, but I am sorry that I didn't tell father and mother before. I cannot undo it and make it as I wish it had been, but I am glad, however, that they were willing to forgive and God has buried it beneath the crimson tide. Praise His name!

CHAPTER III

OFF FOR CHICAGO

I had a strange leading to attend Bible School at Chicago. My wife had corresponded with them some, in fact, had been accepted before we were married. In marrying when we did, we had figured from an economic standpoint, in that it would be cheaper for us to go to school together rather than separately. However, I was not receiving any encouragement from my district superintendent, for he was doing his best to dissuade me. My parents, too, were very much opposed and along with all of these handicaps, the family purse was very low.

We had both been accepted and had written that we would be there for the fall term, early in September, but how we were to go we did not know. The old Ford had been faithful, even to blowing out a tire occasionally, but Chicago was like the other side of the globe and we could never drive there. Our money was small but our faith was smaller, however, God was on the throne and teaching us to trust as a mother teaches her child to walk.

Finally I told my wife that I was going to order the tickets which I did. They came to a little over $59.00 and had to be gotten Friday. The trunks were to go on Saturday and we were to go the next week. On Wednesday, I did my best to sell the Ford to a friend but failed. Thursday I was getting desperate;

but not on my knees. All of the time we were washing and packing and getting ready to go. It was Thursday afternoon late, and still no money. I went to prayer but didn't seem to get the ear of God. I came downstairs, and then I thought of a wonderful plan— I would see the man next door. I told him our situation and asked him if he would make me a loan on a personal note. Well he thought he could, and said, "I'll talk it over with my wife and let you know in an hour or so." I was surely happy; told Wife and everything was O. K. In a little while he called me and said, "I am sorry but I guess we can't do it". The bottom fell out of my feeble faith.

Wife and I went to prayer again and told the Lord our troubles, told Him we were whipped, our plans had failed, and we were about to sink unless He undertook. Well, we felt better and went on packing.

About eight o'clock one of my relatives came in, talked awhile and then said, "Floyd, I didn't give you and Linda a wedding present, so thought I would make you a little gift now", and handed me $25.00. "And your Aunt D—— sent you a little gift, too." Then he handed me another envelope with $25.00 in it. Glory to God! We almost went straight up. It was almost unbelievable but there were the greenbacks.

The next day a dear old saint of God, who went to Heaven recently, handed my wife $10.00. Well there it was; $59.00 and some cents were needed and the Lord had sent us $60.00. I think our faith reached ninety degrees in the shade, but only to be tried a little later.

On Sunday we went to the little church where I had preached my first sermon. It held a tender place in my memory. It was only about ten months before that they called me, but how I had learned to love the people. Not a great distance away was the house where my sweetheart and I took dinner the day we settled the question; down below the pasture and the old fence where we had stood when we decided the time for our union. All of this was dear to our memory, but God was leading; He had corroborated the fact by supplying just in time. I preached my farewell sermon and with tears and good old Methodist handshakes we parted.

Well it was Monday. The church had made me a present of $25.00 and we were more than anxious for Wednesday to arrive. I received a telephone call from my friend W——, saying that he would buy the Ford; I should leave it in the garage and he would meet me at the train and give me $125.00. Well, I could have shouted, but I had never heard anyone do it, so I didn't.

All this while my parents, with whom we were staying, had been away. On Monday they returned. I suppose father thought all the talk about Chicago was like so many rattles on old Lizzy, but when he saw everything in readiness to move, he wanted to know what it all meant. "Going to Chicago, Papa." "Chicago!" I guess he wondered if it had rained dollars while they were away, for he knew that we had but little money. My salary at the church had been $350.00 per year. He was certainly disgusted; I guess he wondered what we would be trying next.

He wanted to know why we had to go 1000 miles away from home to go to school. Well, I couldn't tell him only that I felt led to do it, which was as so much Greek to him, as he was an unsaved man.

Wednesday morning arrived and my pocketbook was in possession of $15.00. But I was not worrying for I would soon have $125.00 more. Father, mother and brother drove us to Philadelphia to the station and there we parted. Poor mother, I know how she must have felt, for a thousand miles from home to mother's heart was like going to China. I can see her now as she said to wife, "Now take good care of my boy".

It was nearly train time and W—— had not arrived with that $125.00. Just as we walked out to the gates, I saw a tall slim fellow, mostly legs, coming across the platform. I recognized it as W——. My hopes rose again. "Is it train time?" he gasped, trying to recover from his long walk and great haste. "Well Brad", he ejaculated, "I'm sorry." And then the thermometer of hope rapidly dropped to zero. I waited. "Dad has been keeping my money for me and refused to give it to me to buy the Ford", but with the next breath he shoved his hand into his pockets and drew out an envelope and said, "Here is a gift for you, and may God bless you!" We shook hands like old pals and through the gate we went.

We found our way to our seats and after some time got our baggage arranged. The train was moving and wife was wiping the tears. The thoughts of the trip stirred her emotions. There was something else stirring me; not my emotions, but my curiosity. I had been stunned and my expectations had received quite a blow at not receiving the $125.00, and I was anxious to see how substantial a gift my friend W—— had put into the envelope. I took it out and there was but $5.00. Someone says, "Be thankful for that." I was, but when I had planned on $125.00 and received only $5.00 it meant that I would have to do quite a bit of calculation to make ends meet, for I knew that at Chicago I would meet a board bill for the first month of about $50.00. However, as the train rolled on our feeble faith took hold and His strong arm undergirded us and we laid every care at His feet.

A colored man with a shining face and white coat was at our elbow. "What could I get fo yous?" I was surprised. "Why, I didn't want anything." Did yous ring dat bell?" Wife said, "I—I guess I did." "Did you want something to eat, Dear?" I could see it was all Greek to her. Everybody was looking, I was embarrassed and I guess she was. My old pride was rebelling against such a scene as that, so in spite of the financial predicament we were in, I ordered some cold drinks and got rid of that black boy as soon as possible. When folks in the car had turned their attention to their books, papers, etc, wife said, "I didn't know that was a bell button and I pushed it. Why didn't you tell me?" I said, "Why didn't you tell me you were going to push it?" Well the cold drinks took fifty cents right out of the family purse and didn't help to cool my carnal pride a bit.

We landed in Pittsburgh and had about two hours to wait for train connections. It was supper time so

we went out to a restaurant and had something to eat
and then walked around and viewed the city. "Why
look there!" exclaimed my wife. I looked hurriedly
and by that time she was walking me up to a jewelry
store window. "Look at those beautiful rings! Why,
Dear, they look just like real diamonds, and they are
only two dollars!" She had always wanted a diamond
and I had never been able to afford one, so we became
engaged without it. I wanted to do something to
please her for I knew she was sort of homesick and
then, too, I had hurt her feelings over pushing that
button and making me spend that unnecessary money.
Poor dear, she wanted to be in style and I wanted her
to, so in we went and purchased a $2.00 diamond
ring. We made up our mind that we would squeeze
all of the other $2.00 to make up for it. I wonder at
the great patience of God with us poor ignoramuses.

We had had a partial night's sleep in the berth or
at least I had; every time I awoke wife was looking
out the window for fear she would miss something
or that something wouldn't miss us. It was morning
and we were dressing when wife reached down under
the berth for her shoes. "Oh!" she said, "someone
has stolen my brand new shoes." "Be quiet, Dear,
don't you know the porter takes them to shine them
for us?" "Well they didn't need shining; they are
new and anyway suppose he would get them mixed
with someone's else." I know folks in the other berth
heard her and this surely mortified my "old man".
To think she would tell everybody in the car that she
had never ridden in a sleeper before. The shoes came
back, however, and that was over.

We pulled into Chicago about 8:45 A. M. and after getting all our luggage together, managed to get off and start for the waiting room. Did I say luggage? Well it was almost enough for an express man; in fact I felt like one. I wouldn't think of letting my wife carry anything but a little package and I took the rest. The rest consisted of two suitcases, (one full of books) and a traveling bag, a violin case, an unbrella, a hat-bag and a camera. I presume I looked like a moving van. The crowd was pushing me from side to side and the porters were pestering me on every hand. I guess I looked as though I needed help—well I did, but I needed my money worse. The perspiration was dripping from my face and the carnal mind was growing very feverish under the pressure, especially with folks smiling at my *"few parcels"*.

I saw a sign "Restaurant". I was not going by outward signs, but there was an inward sign that I needed something to eat if I expected to go far with that load. We went in, I was hot and blue, and glad to find a place to put my luggage down. I piled it up by a table and dropped into a chair. I grumbled some about so much luggage, sat there thinking it over when the waiter touched me on the shoulder and said, "Will you kindly remove your hat?" "Hat"! I grabbed it off quickly. Another blow to my pride; I felt like everyone was looking at me, lost my appetite at once and was anxious to get out of that place. I thought to myself, We are acting worse than two country hayseeds.

We got our little bite, grabbed up the baggage and were off. We struggled down the street for a square.

They were calling, "Cab", "Cab", "Yellow Cab", and someone was all the while trying to carry my bags for me. It was bad enough to have such a load without someone trying to get them away from me. I didn't know where to go, what car to take or how to get to the school. I had all that information in a catalogue but it was packed in one of those troublesome suitcases. Feeling very much agitated over everything, I don't suppose I was very pleasant. Wife was trailing along with her $2.00 diamond ring. "Bang!" One suitcase left my hand and struck the ground—the one with the books in it. The handle had pulled out. This was the climax. "There", I ejaculated, "I told you that wouldn't hold! What am I going to do now? Too much luggage anyway for two people! I don't know why we had to bring so much!" At this I was ready to spend the last penny I had to get relief. A taxi stood near, so I beckoned the driver and he relieved me of my luggage and piled them in the front and we climbed in the back.

Off we went like a shot; through traffic, in and out, up side streets, under elevated railroads, across boulevards, out onto wide business streets, seemingly stopping for nothing. First a narrow escape here, and then there; squeeking of brakes, tooting of horns, etc. After a wild ride of about twenty minutes we drove up in front of the school. We got out and the driver piled our luggage on the sidewalk and asked for 90c. Wife said, "I wouldn't pay it. That's robbery!" I looked at her in disgust; after the man had saved us from our dilemma, made an express truck out of his cab, gotten us to the school without broken necks, and then begrudge him ninety cents!

After some difficulties we got settled in a nice room, received our instructions and were told to go to the accounting department and we could pay our bill. I had just about $15.00 so said I'd go and apply it immediately on our board before something came along to take it. To my surprise, I had forgotten several small fees that had to be paid in addition. I paid them amounting to $12.00 and still could pay nothing on the board bill. I took a step of faith and said that I would have it in three days, but I had not the slightest idea where it would come from. That very day a married couple who were attending the school, whose parents we knew in New Jersey, came to our room and said the Lord had told them to give us $25.00 that they had laid away. Well, what a stimulant to our faith or rather a real rejuvenation! By the third day we received a check for $29.00 from a concern for which I had worked; with these two amounts we were able to pay our bill and have a few dollars besides.

We began our classes which consumed our mornings and were very fortunate in getting work for the afternoons, or rather God provided us with it. The expenses for both were nearly $14.00 per week and we were making about $21.00 between us; so we had much to be thankful for.

We had been in Chicago about two months. Everything was going fine, needs were being met, and prosperity was predominating. During this time we had come to the conclusion that since we were in the Lord's work, or rather in preparation, it was not necessary for us to tithe our income, so we didn't.

One morning wife said she was sick. It meant no school and no work that day. It went several days and still no improvement. The doctor, after a few days, diagnosed her case as serious and said nothing would help but an operation and he did not promise recovery. This was an awful blow, only married about five months and now to have my companion snatched away so soon. We talked it over and finally she decided that she would go. Of course, with little encouragement from the doctor, we talked over everything of importance.

We had a bill that had been standing for several months, one that had to be paid. We had promised the Lord if He would help us get the $40.00 together we would use it for that alone. We had just $40.00. Should I keep it for any emergency that would arise? Wife said, "No, pay it and let us trust God." I did and that afternoon took her to the hospital.

I was surely downcast; what should I do? A thousand miles from home, wife in the hospital with little hope offered, and not a penny to my name. I had a letter in my pocket to her father and not even a stamp to mail it. As I trudged along in a very despondent mood my eyes caught sight of a stamp. I picked it up and to my surprise it was a good one. Thank the Lord. It was only worth 2c but it encouraged me. All I needed just then was a stamp and God had it there when I needed it. Amen! If He could meet my need of a stamp, and just when I needed it, He could meet every other need.

The day of the operation arrived and one of the men from the school, a Brother F——, went to the hospital with me. We had prayer with my dear companion, they lifted her on the carrier and away she went to the operating room on the next floor. What an anxious hour I spent! Brother F——, God bless him, was such a comfort. How he did talk to me and quoted passage after passage of Scripture while the grace of God kept lifting me. At last they brought her out and took her to the room. Oh, what a relief to know that she was still alive. For several days she suffered intensely, but then began to be herself and improved **rapidly.**

In about two weeks she was able to go home, but instead of going back to live at the school we thought it better to get a light housekeeping room so that she could have the food she liked and wouldn't have to climb the stairs back and forth from the dining room. This was all settled and we located just across from the school.

The next thing was the hospital bill. How could we pay it? It amounted to a little more than $70.00. The school obligated themselves to pay half of it but where would I get the other half. I was working in the afternoons to be sure, but only making $10.50 per week and was paying $8.00 for room rent. Instead of things opening up for us they became worse. Time went on, the hospital was waiting for their money and everything flat, purse included. Finally I said to my wife, "I believe I have the secret of our trouble. We haven't tithed since we came here. I'm going to give my tenth if I don't have anything left." When

Saturday came, I took $1.05 out of my $10.50, paid $8.00 to the landlady and gave wife $1.45 to live on for the week. "Well," she said, "I'll pray that God will help me make it reach."

Thinking that nothing would be so economical as a pot of vegetable soup, she purchased a bone and a few vegetables and placed them just outside the window intending to make soup the next day. We were on the ground floor, but there were bars around the window so thought it would be safe. In the morning we arose with our mouths in soup fashion; wife went to get the bone and behold all that was left was the paper and it was torn and scratched. Poor dear, she sat down and cried; I got up and stormed. If I could have found the dog I'm afraid I would have either lost my religion or gotten bit, perhaps both.

The next evening, still planning on stretching that $1.45, she thought that a corn-starch pudding would be cheap and yet nourishing; we were both fond of it, so she got busy. When it was all finished I said, "Now I'll set it out to cool". So I took it out in the hall near the door and set it up high and dry on a milk bottle. Wife got everything else ready for supper and we sat down, thinking we would leave the pudding in the hall until we were ready so that it would be good and solid. We were perhaps half through when the door opened and in an instant—crash! "Oh, my!" I jumped to my feet and made for the hall. I found the pudding; it was spread from one side to the other; some careless boy had ruined our hopes again. Talk about the crash in Wall Street. This was equally as bad to us in our hard circum-

stances. I didn't say much to that boy, but I felt like
it. Well, it did seem like we were in hard straits.
With all of the misfortune I don't see how $1.45 ran
our table all week, but it did. Praise the Lord! We
decided if it would one week when we tithed it would
every week; so we continued.

About the middle of the next week, still looking to
God earnestly for money to pay the hospital bill, we
received a strange letter from Philadelphia. I tore
it open and something blue fell out. I looked and it
was a money order to F. N. B. "Fifty—fifty cents I
guess." "Let me see", said my wife and she grabbed
it. "No, fifty dollars." "Fifty dollars!" I exclaimed.
We looked at it together and sure enough it was. Then
we got our bearings and read the letter. It was from
a man by the name of Mr. T—— to whom I had loaned
some money the year before I was married.

I had hired a lawyer to get it for me; Mr. T—— had
really gotten it from me under false pretense, but the
lawyer had failed to assist us. Praise God He knew
when I would need it most and here it was just in
time. We paid the bill and some other incidentals
and had a little to help us run our table for the next
couple of weeks.

I was called in the school employment office one day
and told that I could get a room in another house for
$4.00 providing I would look after the furnace night
and morning, carry out all the ashes and carry in all
the coal. Well I went and investigated. It meant
quite a bit of work for $4.00 per week, but we needed
the money, so I said, "All right." The only handicap
was that we would have to cook with an electric stove

and that would mean an investment of eight dollars, but we figured we would make that up in a little while; so we moved.

We had just gotten settled, paid out $8.00 for the stove when to my surprise I was laid off at the Department Store. What a blow! However we had a couple of dollars and made them do the week out.

It was Saturady night and very close inventory of our cupboard showed coffee, a few slices of bread, about enough dried lima beans for two helpings and a can of Dutch Cleanser. Our cash balance on hand was O. What a predicament! I had never been in such a shape before and hoped I never would again. How we did think about the folks back East, but that only tended to make matters worse, so we dropped such thoughts and began to trust. We had our devotions and crawled into bed, awoke in the morning to eat some bread and black coffee for breakfast, and by mutual agreement we decided to save the beans for the noon meal.

I had an assignment for Sunday morning to teach a Sunday School class in Eggelston, but only had one car ticket; a way to go but no way to get back. I could use but one ticket to go so, that was all I needed until it was time to return. After prayer I said I'd venture out on faith; bade wife good-bye and started for Eggelston. I taught my class. The school was dismissed and no one handed me a cent. I confess I went down the street toward the elevated feeling that my faith was weakening. However, I climbed the stairs and stood there wondering what to do next. I had gone as far as I could, there was the turnstile and it took a ticket or a dime to go through. "Hello, Bradley, going home?" said a voice behind me. "Why— why—yes", I stammered and by that time a little English fellow had me by the arm, dropped two tickets on the window and pushed me through. It was several minutes before I could get myself together. What a wonderful God; just what I needed, and no more, no less. Praise His name!

I hurried home as fast as I could to tell my companion how God had worked it all out and she praised the Lord with me. I was home but a few minutes until she had dinner ready. Excuse me—I mean she had our beans on the table, bread and black coffee to match. After such an experience we felt thankful for what we had and I don't believe I ever ate such good beans before nor since. In the evening, we finished the bread, went to church, came home hungry and went to bed empty to forget our predicament.

Monday morning we became desperate. Having no school, we borrowed a paper from one of the women in the house and decided to find a job or know the reason why. We left home quite early and walked a good two miles to the Loope Section and answered several ads but with no avail; our efforts seemed to mock us. We were tired, hungry, cold, and wife was half sick, not having been out of the hosital more than two months.

After awhile we met a Miss A——; she was delighted to see us; wanted to know if we were shopping. "No, just looking around," we said. She was going to do some and wanted us to go along. We had nothing else to do and nothing to go home for so we trailed along rather dejected looking, I imagine. My, how that woman did spend the money and a great deal for non-essentials, all the time asking my wife why she didn't get so and so. Well, we knew why, but determined we wouldn't say a word to anyone. After Miss A—— had walked us from counter to counter, and store to store, until wife looked like she would sink to the floor and I felt like it, she said, "Well, it's noon and I am hungry." We said nothing. Several times she made the remark, but still we said nothing. "Well, I'll take you to dinner," she said. That was what we had been hoping for. She led the way down the street to a drug store, into the basement, and we seated ourselves at one of the tables. I didn't think it looked much like a place to get a dinner, but still said nothing. The waiter came. "I'm going to have a ham sandwich and a cup of coffee," she said. My heart sank, my stomach growled. Wife and I mutually agreed to have the same, but rather reluctantly.

After "dinner" was over we walked around some, thanked Miss A—— for her hospitality and started home. It was about two miles but I believe those ham sandwiches were the subject of our conversation all the way.

We were near the school and wife suggested that we stop and see if there was any mail. It was about two squares out of our way and I objected; but she insisted so we went. To her delight and my surprise there was a letter. "It's from Aunt I——," she said and tore it open. Out rolled three one dollar bills. Well, we laughed and cried all at once. What a time we had; we went up the street as fast as we could walk and stopped at the first store we came to. That meant as much to our faith as a hypodermic to a dying man. Between sobs wife told the man what she wanted, one half dozen eggs, package of bacon, loaf of bread, etc. Oh, my, what a spread we would have. We hustled home and it wasn't long before the grease was spattering and the eggs were crackling in the pan. We surely did pray over that meal and sang the Doxology too.

Along about nine o'clock, a distant relative of mine, who lived in Chicago and whom we had visited several times, called on the telphone. Wife went down the hall and answered it and came back with her face aglow. B——'s husband had a job for me; office work, not hard, would pay $40.00 per week and they would advance me two weeks' salary if I needed it. What a proposition! What about my schooling? Wife suggested that I could transfer to the evening course. "Yes, I could do that." We were to call her in the morning, so that gave a little time to think it over. It did look big but I'm satisfied it would have looked a great deal bigger had I not had that good meal of bacon and eggs an hour or so before.

I'll never forget that night; I stayed up most of it and prayed earnestly. It was a crisis I felt. God showed me my downfall if I took it. It was settled. I'd trust God to open up something else where I could continue my schooling during the day. I told wife the next morning what I had decided; she has said since that she thought me foolish at the time but made no reply.

We had not exhausted our three dollars when I had a position to work in the evenings and would draw

$17.00 per week. Wife had one during the day and received a salary of $23.00 per week, which just amounted to $40.00 the same as I was offered by Mr. B——. Praise the dear Lord. He will see us through if we will trust Him.

"Trust and obey, for there's no other way,
To be happy in Jesus, but to trust and obey."

About this time one of the students who had a pastorate was leaving school and hunting someone to take his place. It was about forty miles from Chicago in a Free Methodist Church. He was in the habit of going down over the week-end. He spoke to me about it and I jumped at the chance. He told me it was a Free Methodist Church, but that didn't mean anything to me. I didn't know the difference between a Free Methodist and a "tied-up" Methodist. It was all arranged and I was getting ready to go to Shelby, Indiana. I got out my long-tailed coat, shined up my watch chain, put my diamond pin in my necktie and fixed up like a real preacher and took the train Sunday morning for Shelby.

I arrived O. K. and a kindly old man met me and directed me up to the church. I sat in the back until Sunday School was out and then in a dignified, professional manner mounted the rostrum, dropped on one knee for about ten seconds and opened the service. I had carefully sorted over my sermons and chosen the two best ones for the day and, unconscious of the people to whom I was preaching and ignorant of the doctrines of the church, I waxed eloquent. Then again

at night I did my best. I was candidating for the pulpit. Needless to tell you I never heard from them
from that day till this. I noticed they looked me over
very closely, but I thought they were admiring my
beautiful scarf pin or my dignified manners. Well, the
old adage was true, "Where ignorance is bliss, 'tis
folly to be wise."

CHAPTER IV

A YEAR IN THE CATSKILLS

After returning from Chicago because of wife's health, we were at a loss to know what to do. Our first intentions were to stay in the East awhile, earn some money, and then return to Bible School to finish our course; but God in His great plan directed us in a different way, working things together for our good and His own glory.

I pottered around, working at several different things, preaching wherever the opportunity afforded and doing secular work during the week. After about three months we happened to get in touch with a church, about fifteen miles from home, which was closed and had no pastor. We looked into the matter, found out that there were about two members living and, with their consent, we opened the church. We will not forget that first Sunday morning. There were cobwebs in the corners, dirt on the floor, dust on the pews, and a congregation of three. Two men, who were quite deaf, and one woman. We were glad, however, for a place to be in action if it were a soap box. I preached away to the three and to my good wife who nodded her approval occasionally and gave me some encouragement.

It was a good community for a church. There was only this one near, so we set out to visit the homes and acquainted the folks with the fact that we were open for business. We continued working during the week in the city and going to our appointments on Sundays. Sometimes the offering would be twenty-five cents, sometimes fifty cents; but with an increase in attendance nearly every Sunday, there was an incentive to keep at it. We stayed until conference time which was a period of about four months. The last Sunday the attendance was nearly a hundred, and the outlook was good for the next year.

Of course we went to conference with a glowing report and chest out and to our surprise we were offered a church in the Catskill Mountains. There was quite a novelty in having a call to a place where we had never been, and the doctor had said I had better get into a higher altitude; so we embraced the opportunity and accepted the call.

Going so far away and to a semi-rural section, we immediately felt the need of a car. The conference had given us some money for traveling expenses so, with that and hoping for more, we planned on getting a Ford. Though hoping and praying, we were surprised when nearly two hundred dollars came in from various sources. Needless to say we bought the car, made a good payment down, and were ready for the trip.

About five o'clock, one morning in October, with the car loaded with dishes, etc., a dog in the back seat and three of us in the front seat, including wife's father whom we had persuaded to go to live with us, we turned the little Ford touring car toward the Catskills. We drove all day, part of the time through a pouring rain, got lost in the mountains on back roads,

nearly slipped over an embankment, and finally landed
in a lumber camp about sixty miles from our destination, at nine o'clock at night. We received directions
and went on, and arrived in the vicinity of the little
village of F—— with three tired passengers, a weary
dog, and a new Ford hardly limbered up after a seven-
teen-hour trip.

We stopped at the first house that showed a light
and rapped at the door. It opened, and the glimmer
of a lamp threw its rays across the porch. We were
in the land of the living after all.

A kindly voice from the little grey-haired woman
asked if I was the new minister and upon reply she
said we had better put up there for the night. We
were willing, so the weary four, dog and all, filed in
and found a comfortable cozy retreat for the night.

We awoke in the morning and gazed out on a beautiful scene. The mountains were rich with the bril-
liant colors of autumn, while the azure sky and bright
sun made the picture complete. When breakfast was
over, being anxious to see the parsonage, Brother
A—— took us down the road to the village which consisted of a store, church, and perhaps twenty houses,
with the beautiful Catskills on either side. We then
went to the parsonage, standing alone just beyond the
village on the side of a high hill. We lost no time
going in and—what a place! It was a nice house,
beautifully situated, but had been poorly kept by its
former occupants. For two months we spent our time
cutting down brush, cleaning, painting, papering, etc.

On Sunday morning we were greeted by a congregation of perhaps fifty, mostly farmers, and somewhat

"sot" in their ways. I preached one of my best sermons to them and got acquainted.

We had not been used to extremely cold weather in New Jersey, so did not know how to prepare for it. We had not been used to wood fires, nor burning green wood, so had no idea what was before us. We had not been used to oil lamps and hardly knew how to work them. We had not been used to a cistern and did not know that the water came from the roof. We had not been used to country cookstoves and so did not know where to find the reservoir, and wife was walking all around the house with a bucket of water looking for it. What a time! It was like learning to live all over again. We both had been born and reared in the city and knew nothing of life in a rural section.

One night, to our surprise, the mercury went to twenty degrees below zero, and the next day was Sunday. We all came downstairs and found that both fires were out and there was only green wood to burn. The pump was frozen, the water bucket was frozen, the tea-kettle was frozen, and so were we. The trio donned the heaviest coats we had and attempted to get things thawed out. I think for almost an hour we burned about as much oil as we did wood, pouring it in a can time after time to get the fire under way. We finally got some breakfast cooked and sat down to eat it, dressed like Eskimos, stopping every few bites to rub our hands and warm them. It is not necessary to say that we had very few out to church that morning.

One morning wife said, "Dear, this is all the wood we have" and put several sticks in the stove. I knew it, but had decided that I would not run in debt for it. We sat down to breakfast, bowed our heads and started to return thanks, but were led off to pray for wood, telling the Lord how badly we needed it. Before I had finished the door-bell rang. Upon opening it I was greeted by Mr. S—— with a load of fine seasoned wood all sawed and split, perhaps three cords in all. Praise God! does He not say, "Before you call, I will answer, and while you are yet speaking I will hear"? Our faith surely took a new grip on the precious promises.

During my minstry at F—— I began to see my need of more grace than I had in my possession. The Lord helped me in preparing my sermons but occasionally I would have a bad spell of ill temper which would throw me under a dense cloud for several days. Sometimes it would be over the green wood, sometimes over wife's displeasing me, and sometimes over the Ford.

One rather cold morning, as I was to have a funeral service at eleven o'clock and had a sermon to prepare, I decided after breakfast that I had better get the car running and warmed up first, and then prepare the message. I went to the barn around nine o'clock with several pails of hot water, a determination to start the Ford, and a fair measure of grace. It was a model "T" and having had similar experiences with it, I knew about what to do. I followed the usual routine, pouring hot water on the manifold, filling the radiator, jacking up the rear-end, etc. With all this done, I began to crank. I cranked and cranked and c-r-a-n-k-e-d, and C-R-A-N-K-E-D. I cranked the skin off my hands, and it would not go. I cranked myself breathless, and it would not go. I cranked myself weary, and it would not go. I cranked all the grace out of my heart and there was not even a spark. Then I cranked myself cranky—and exploded; some folks call it flying off the handle. I lay against the front fender, breathless and graceless; I would have sold that Ford to the first fellow that had made me an offer at that moment.

I went to the house disgusted; told wife that a Ford was nothing for a preacher anyway; but I found later that it wasn't the Ford so much as it was the "old man" in my heart. Wife had been suffering with an infected toe, but I persuaded her to go out to the barn and help me push "Lizzy" out. We did, and with the help of the starter got it to where the road pitched down. My idea was that if I could run it down the hill from the house to the road, I'd be sure to get it started. I climbed in and wife gave a little push to start it rolling, but she forgot to take her sore toe out of the way. I ran over it and that caused her to explode. Down the hill I went. I got on level ground and stopped, but never a grunt from "Lizzy".

Wife hobbled down after she had gotten over the explosion and her toe felt better. I had her climb in and I cranked. "Choke it", "Pull the gas down", "Put the spark up", I shouted. With all my directions she got nervous and didn't know the spark from the gas. Right opposite where my car was standing lived a man who ran the village garage, but whose rates were quite expensive and I had made it a practice of going to M—— for repairs. I had cranked and cranked for perhaps ten minutes more and was tired and dirty and exceedingly carnal. I happened to look up and saw him standing in the window laughing at me. This climaxed all—no, I didn't say anything, but what I thought! I pushed the car to the side of the road and helped my poor wife, with her sore toe, up to the house.

I wasn't more than half dressed when someone rapped at the door furiously and wanted to know if the preacher wasn't coming to the funeral. I fell into my clothes, grabbed my funeral book and was off to bury the dead. I do not know what I said at that service. I am sure I was not in any mood to preach.

It was early summer, and we had planned to go to Albany and take Brother and Sister E—— with us. I had a new straw hat but thought it was too early to wear it. Wife insisted that I put it on, telling me how bad my old one looked. After she insisted and coaxed, I wore it. We stopped for our passengers and went on; we had gone quite a distance when a gust of wind took my hat off and rolled it down the road into some nice fresh tar, and it gathered it up as it rolled. "There, I told you I didn't want to wear it," I said to my wife. Then I remembered that we had someone in the back seat, and climbed out without further comment. Sister E——, in her quiet way, had her hand to her face to hide a smile. I got the hat and tried to wipe the tar off, but it was hopeless. The hat was ruined, and so was my reputation. There! I had exploded right before the best members in the church.

Sister E—— was a quiet saintly woman, always the same, nothing seemed to ruffle her. How my heart longed for such an experience! I felt like a hungry little street urchin looking on while another boy devours a bag of cookies. Truly this dear sister's life was a testimony of sanctifying grace.

It was early spring and my dear grandmother was visiting us. She had lived on a farm most of her life, so felt right at home in such a place. One afternoon she said she would make some hot muffins for supper. That was fine; we set our mouths accordingly. She had them all ready but couldn't get the fire to burn. *More green wood.* "Well, children", she said, "I've burned many a stick of wood but never saw anything like this." Wife worked with it and tried to coax it along, but with no success. How it did smoke and smoulder! The kitchen was full of smoke and so were Grandma's eyes. Pour soul, the tears were just running down her cheeks. Yes, the muffins were in, but that's about all. I made up my mind that I'd make it burn, so began to administer first aid by means of kerosene, a can full at a time, and with a great deal of carnal determination. Finally my temper had gotten to a white heat. To think that some of the folks made their brags that they had enough seasoned wood to last them four years and they were too stingy to give the preacher some. I went to the phone and cranked that old farmers' line in good shape. Mr. K——, one of the stewards, answered. I told him, in a rather heated manner, the circumstances and said, "If you don't have some seasoned wood here for me tomorrow, I'm leaving for New Jersey", and hung up. I felt better after I had gotten that off my heart; but as I thought about it, I felt worse. There, see how

I had acted, and me the preacher; another explosion! O God, if I could only get to a place where I'd have control over such a temper.

We sat down to supper and ate dried-out dough for muffins and whatever else we had. I wasn't hungry; except my soul. I wanted an experience that would keep me sweet under all circumstances. I believed God could do it for me but how would I go about getting it? After such an outburst, I would spend most of my time in the study for a day or two praying and crying. God would hear me and forgive my sin; and immediately getting restored to a justified state, I would feel better, and think I had the victory over my temper, only to find in a few weeks that I was still in possession of that inward foe.

After supper I went down the road to see Brother K——. I called him outside and tried to patch things up. He loaded the back of my car with wood and home I went. The next morning about ten o'clock someone drove in the yard with a load of nice seasoned wood. Before it was unloaded wife looked down the road and said, "Here comes J—— with a load of wood. I believe he is coming here". And he did. It was not many minutes until Grandma looked up the road and said, "Why, children, someone just turned in the driveway with another load of wood." My spell was carnal, and I had a job repenting over it; but it brought in about six cords of wood.

During the summer we had some dear folks visit us, and Sister W—— talked much about the deeper things of God. She told about a presiding elder who had carnal spells every time there was a stove to be put up, and how God wonderfully delivered him from it so that stoves or nothing else troubled him. I listened with eager heart and determined that I would have it also, and went to work diligently trying to obtain it by growth. No doubt I grew some but not into this experience, as it is a definite work of grace. However, I kept at it only to find that I had an eruption now and then; sometimes outward, and sometimes inward, but with great difficulty to hold it down.

Someone gave us some hens. We had twelve and one rooster. Wife didn't know a thing about them only where to find the eggs when she needed some. No doubt she had heard someone say that a certain shaped egg would produce a rooster; she, no doubt, had taken it all in and formed her own conclusions. One evening I came in elated, "Why, dear, we got thirteen eggs today", I said. She made some comment and went on preparing supper. A few days later we were in company with some of the church members, and the subject of eggs was brought up. Some were speaking of how well their hens were laying, when to my surprise, wife said "Why even our rooster lays." They surely did laugh, but she was serious. When things were quiet, she told them that we had twelve hens and a rooster and they had all laid for we got thirteen eggs in one day. You can readily see that our experience in the Catskills was all brand new.

In September a certain evangelist, who lived a few miles away, began holding tent meetings in his home town. We had heard him once, what a sermon he gave and with such power behind it! I had never heard anything like it before, and how it gripped my heart! Wife did not like him nor his sermon; she said it scared her and she didn't want to hear him again. Of course we didn't know that he was a Holiness preacher. I don't suppose we would have known what they meant if they had told us.

When we heard of these meetings, I persuaded wife to go, so we attended about every night. I knew there was something that he possessed that I did not, nor the average preacher, but I did not know it by name nor how it was acquired. We were at the altar several nights, with other church folks and the town preacher, but didn't know what it was all about. I don't know whether he preached a second blessing sermon or not; if he did, I did not grasp it. Strange to say I never linked it up with the experience for which I had been hungering. It does not seem to me, as I look back, that it was God's time for the light to break in upon me. All of these things were no doubt preparing the soil of my heart to await God's own time.

The year was coming to a close and, being in a carnal state, I was not so much concerned about doing God's will as I was about pleasing myself, or rather, I let carnal desires decide the will of God for me. Be it as it may, we were tired of green wood, carrying our drinking water, and trying to crack some old hard shells, so I decided to resign.

The last quarterly conference took place and all of the business was transacted except the calling of the preacher for the new year, I turned the chair over to one of the officials and left the room. Upon my return I was told that I had a unanimous vote to return as pastor for the coming year. In substance I replied that I felt they were not receptive to the truth, and the Bible distinctly said we should not cast our pearls before swine; and though I appreciated the unanimous call, I would not return. I wonder how I said such without a blush of embarrassment, but carnality can do a great deal without blushing.

CHAPTER V

MOVED, BUT IN TWO WAYS

It was beautiful Autumn weather, and we were cozily situated in our new apartment. We were on a new field, near our relatives and friends, no wood fires to look after, stores within walking distance and everything convenient. It seemed as if we would have a good year on our new charge in New Jersey.

Just a few weeks after we were settled, the denomination was having a district convention about forty miles from our home. It was to be held on Friday and every preacher was to bring a delegate from his charge. I had arranged to take a Mr. J——, a big man in the church and a big man in size, but with little religion, as I found out afterward.

On Thursday night we had planned to attend a meeting under the direction of Rev. T. M. Anderson and Dr. Mingeldorf, held in a church about eight miles from home. We went as planned; and, of course being acquainted with the pastor, we were invited to the pulpit, shook hands with the evangelists and made the opening prayer. We had noticed, on the bulletins advertising the meetings, that they were "The Holiness Flying Squadron". This was new to us, and we wondered why they should call themselves "Holiness". That was a strange word to our ears and caused us to look on curiously to see what would take place next. We had never heard the pastor speak of "Holiness" and, by his life, we did not think he had any more religion than the average; however, we made up our mind we would be open and receptive and see what would be given out.

It was Brother Anderson's turn to preach that evening, and after some brief preliminaries he arose and began his discourse. The longer he talked the more earnest he became and the more interested I became. He was painting some pictures. At first it was the "Natural Man" and then it was the "Carnal Man". When he had finished this word picture and changed his brushes to continue, I recognized that he had given a perfect word picture of myself. I looked at my wife, but she was not feeling well and did not seem to be taking it in; I was glad for once that she wasn't. Then he proceeded with colors of heavenly tone to give us a description of the "Spiritual Man". He surely made every brush mark count, and with what deliberation he portrayed the man who had been freed from the carnal principle. I was located. It seemed that he knew my condition. The light had dawned upon me at last. It was the very thing my soul had been reaching after since I had first knelt at an altar of prayer. My, how I needed it, too, as no doubt you noticed by the preceding chapters.

The invitation was given—I hesitated. One or two went forward. Then there was a more general invitation, and I with others found my way to the front of the church. I did not go with tears; my emotions were not stirred in the least. I had been living up to all the light I had and like a man making a business deal, I got on my knees and thanked God for the message, the light, took Him at His word and felt satisfied that the work was done. Of course this, I know, would not harmonize very well with the pet notions of some, nor would they be able to pour me into their mould; but I knew God had heard me. The meeting was out; wife was half sick; and I was sanctified. I had not only moved back to New Jersey but into Canaan Land.

We waited inside the church door for quite a while for my brother who was to be there to meet us at nine-thirty. He had borrowed our Ford and promised faithfully to return on time. The janitor wanted to close the church, so we decided to take a street car and go to my parents, but a short distance away, and wait until he came home. We arrived in a few minutes and there we sat from about ten until midnight, and no Wesley yet. My wife being sick and carnal, besides, was grumbling every few minutes and getting ready to open fire on him when he came. About twelve-thirty he rolled in the driveway. Wife and he exchanged some charges of T. N. T. but strange to say I felt as meek as a lamb.

We climbed in and started for home; we had not gone more than twenty-five yards when I noticed that "Lizzy" seemed to be limping like an old man with gout. *"Flat tire!* I guess". I climbed out and sure enough there it was and made no apologies for its presence. I had no jack and what to do I did not know. Then Mrs. B—— exploded the second time. What she would have said to Wesley if she could have seen him then. I said, "Now, dear, we will just make the best of it". I climbed in again and started off slowly, and to my surprise it seemed like they were all flat. Out I climbed the second time, and sure enough there were two. Well, misery likes company. While I stood in back of the car looking the situation over and having a consultation with myself, a good Samaritan drove up and offered his services. It was not long until we were on the road home, and still the precious Dove of Peace was singing in my soul. Praise God! We were nearly home and just about five hundred yards from the apartment when pop—pop— "Lizzy" spit a little and stopped. Out of gas; yes, an old familiar sound. I climbed out again. Wife got into the driver's seat and I put my shoulder to it and pushed the car up to the house. Poor Dear, she was sick in body, angry at Wesley and, as I learned later, wondering why in the world I had gone to the altar and then why I took everything so cool. I went into the house with dirty hands and tired body, but a clean heart, thank God. What a wonderful feeling!

The next morning wife was feeling better, and we were up reasonably early getting ready to go to the convention. We allowed ourselves about one and a half hours to drive the forty miles. We drove around and got our passengers Mr. and Mrs. J—— and away we went in the old Ford. We had not gone more than ten miles or so when there was a very familiar report and "Lizzy" went lame—bump—bump—bump. Just a flat tire, that's all. I climbed out and repaired it, whistling as I worked; Mr. J—— superintended the job. Off we went again and within fifteen or twenty minutes, Bang! another flat. It had gotten quite warm, the sweat was running, and the fire of heavenly love was burning in my soul. In a little while we were on our way; drove perhaps ten miles and another tire called our attention to the fact that it needed repairing. Wife said she didn't think so much about my keeping cool with the first two, but when the third one gave its testimony she thought, Here it goes, and he'll show himself off before our now parishioners and what a time. To her surprise all was well.

I patched and hummed a hymn tune while I worked. In again, and away we went—but not far for we had another flat. "Well, praise the Lord"! and it came from an artesian well of Divine glory in the depth of my soul. Wife thought I must be going to die; surely I was getting too saintly to stay on old mother earth. Four flats and four fixed and the glory still held. I began to marvel at myself; there was no effort on my part and no holding onto my temper. I was certainly proving that the second work of grace, called sanctification, was all the Bible described. Glory to God! No struggle within, just peace—nothing but peace and joy. We climbed in and started, then came number five, then six, and then seven. You must know that we did not get there for the morning service and were late for the afternoon session. The only benefit I derived from the trip was a good chance to prove the Second Blessing.

We went to the parsonage for supper, and when I came out, "Lizzy" greeted me with a FLAT. Well, it was only one, so I fixed it in a hurry.

As my wife was not well we left the evening service early and started for home. We went all the way home, forty miles, and only had one flat tire. I can truthfully say that not once did I feel a stirring within my bosom. I was just as well blessed when I patched the last as the first. What a precious experience, all made possible through the atonement! "Wherefore Jesus also that he might sanctify the people with his own blood, suffered without the gate." Glory to God and the Lamb forever!

The next day was Saturday and wife was not able to be up. I had some preparation yet for Sunday's sermons, storing to do, house to look after and a sick wife; but a sanctified heart revels in testings. The Sabbath arrived and with it my companion in a critical condition. We called a doctor and after examination he said nothing but an operation would help her —if she could stand it.

I left for church that evening. I was thinking, Another operation, no promise of her getting well, and no money except the few dollars I would get from the church for my week's work. In spite of all this, the fire still burned, the glory held, and the joy of the Lord was welling up within my heart and was indeed my strength. Amen! I went into the pulpit, took a text and started to preach, but before I knew it I was off on my new-found experience and how delighted I was with it. Praise God, a preacher that enjoys this can always find something to talk about. The big Mr. J—— was there, and he an old Holiness fighter, but he had to acknowledge that the tire experience was a great demonstration of the keeping grace of God.

We consulted a surgeon for my wife, and he gave very little hope but said he would do his best. She was taken to the hospital for a few days' observation and then the operation. In meditation the Sunday before, wondering if she would get well, this being her sixth operation, she said, "I guess the best place to look for help is in the Bible", and with that she dropped it open. The first text her eyes lighted upon was Job 5:19 "I shall deliver thee in six troubles, yea in seven there shall no evil touch thee". What a promise! What a God! Praise His name! Before daylight, one of the supervisors slipped into the room, saw that wife was awake and put a piece of paper in her hand. She couldn't wait until daylight but at the first glimmer of dawn strained her eyes to see. Just a sentene but much in it. "Underneath are the everlasting arms". Surely they were.

When Dr. T—— opened her, the other doctor said, "Sew her up, T——". "No", he said, "if I do, she will die; I might as well do my best". After three hours on the table she came out of the ether and for several days was on the D. L. and all of the time having serum administered. After five weeks they said she could go home. The doctor came in to see her the day before. "Now, Doctor", she said, "if you will give us your bill, we will do our best to pay it as soon as we are able." "Well," he said, "I don't do much for the church; if my services have been of help, you are welcome to them; there will be no bill". "My God shall supply all of your needs, according to his riches in glory by Christ Jesus". He surely does it. The doctor told one of the nurses that if we had been paying for it, the cost would have been about $1500.00.

We again turned our attention toward our congregation and learned that they were planning to have a church supper. We had always participated in them but now we felt a checking of the Spirit. The Lord plainly showed us that the church was to be a house of prayer and not a soup kitchen. We told them our stand, and it did not meet with their approval; however, we held our ground. It was not more than two months when they were planning a "Sauer Kraut Feed". We objected again but met with much opposition; so the "dogs" and "sauer kraut" had their midwinter frolic. Neither time did we attend, and this was an unusual thing for them not to have the pastor there to shake hands with all of the people; ask God's blessing upon the desecration of His church, and proceed to eat, drink, and be merry.

All of this time we were gaining spiritual momentum; we were learning something of the "Blessing" from a doctrinal standpoint and proving it every day experimentally; both were equipping us more to preach with authority on this great subject. All of the old mules were getting balky and all of the old goats were chewing their filthy weed and bucking like good fellows. The fight was on. With all of this, there was an element in the church that were hungry for the truth, and were growing like weeds in wet weather. This little company of perhaps fifteen or twenty met once a week at the parsonage as a prayer band. We invited no goats, but welcomed all the sheep and young lambs. On one occasion the big Mr. J—— came, but it was too hot for him; he never returned. I love the battle for the cause of righteousness. I had always

been an old "soft soaper" trying to make everybody
love me and speak well of me. Thank God, He had
put something in me that gave me grit and grace
to take my stand and keep blessed while doing it. I
was determined to stand in good at Headquarters, and
I still have the same determination.

The Lord next began to call my attention to the
fact that no doubt they were paying my salary out of
money collected from suppers. I would not attend
and how could I conscientiously take money that was
gotten that way? The next supper came. The Monday following I went to the home of the treasurer to
get my check as usual. "Mr. G.——, are you paying
me out of supper money?" I asked. "Well, part of
it", he replied. "Just give me what came in on Sunday, and I'll be satisfied. I feel condemned to take
money from the suppers." He flushed, tore the check
up and made another one about two-thirds as large.
I thanked him, said good-bye, and went down the
street feeling like Samson when he had gotten honey
out of the carcass of the lion. It was another victory
won, and I felt sweet all over. All the while my dear
companion was standing by me taking her share of
the knocks and bumps and sarcasm.

The next thing it was time for revival meetings. I
tried to work in a Holiness evanglist, but they knew
him and put their foot down solid. Who should we
get? I began praying and God led me to a man,
preaching in a church of the same denomination, quite
a scholarly fellow but full of the Holy Ghost. They
consented, but they didn't know him. The meetings
began after a bit of advertising; the prayer band had

been praying earnestly and the regular prayer services were larger than any church in town and yet we had the smallest membership. Folks were getting converted in the prayer service and others shouting happy. We were in good shape for a meeting. Brother P—— came to us in the fullness of the Blessing. The first two or three nights everyone was carried away with him. I heard them say, "I wonder if we could get him next conference?" I was not taking thought for the morrow. God was blessing me in the present tense, so I hadn't a care. About the fifth or sixth night he began to open fire, and of all the preaching I had ever heard up until that time, it was the greatest. The saints were glad, and the officials were mad, but they did not dare stay at home for fear we would have a free for all time of blessing and that would have been a disgrace to the church. We closed the meeting with victory. A number of the good people had been sanctified and some had been saved, but the officials had changed their minds as to calling Brother P—— for their next pastor.

The closing of the revival effort did not end the "Civil War". It just added fuel to the fire and left us to face the music. The official board, ladies' aid, members, etc., were not the only ones who were having new light thrown across their pathway, but likewise the newly-sanctified pastor. One night while the evangelist was thundering out the truth, I was suddenly conscious of the fact that I had a big, flashy, conspicuous scarf pin bedecking my necktie. Well, I had worn it for several years, and why should it be thrust upon my mind so suddenly—it almost seemed as

though the point was pricking me. Never having
fellowshipped with Holiness people I did not know
their teachings, and strange to say Brother P——
had not mentioned such a thing in his message. One
thing I did know, that God was displeased with the
above-mentioned pin; and the Spirit, not the scarf
pin, was pricking my conscience. I did not hear any
more of the sermon for quite a while. I was having
a confidential talk with F. N. B. When I finished,
the scarf pin was in the back of my coat lapel, instead of in my tie and it has never been in there since.

Another night he was striking pretty close; chips
were flying everywhere, so to speak, and like a thunder
bolt one struck the pastor. My, what now? Well, immediately I had a mental picture of a certain drug
store in the state of Maryland where I had traded.
I could see a twenty-five cent comb as plainly as I
ever had. One time while driving through the town
of C——, I stepped into a drug store to purchase a
comb. The proprietor put several trays of combs on
the case, told me the prices and specified "This one is
unbreakable", pointing to the tray. While I looked
at them, he went to the other side of the store to wait
on another customer. He said it was unbreakable,
and it was stamped on it, so I ventured to test it out,
and to my surprise I had several pieces in my hand.
I did not intend to pay for that after he had misrep-
resented it to me, so I hastily left some of the pieces
slip down between the cases and the other in my
pocket. When he returned I purchased a comb, saying nothing of the broken one. When I saw the comb
in meeting that night it was plain enough. I could

even see *Unbreakable* stamped upon it. I argued some, but I could not get around it, under it, over it, nor through it. Finally, I got at it, and said, "Yes, Lord, I'll make it right", and I did and received a blessing in doing it.

Three months after the revival effort had closed the whole situation reached a climax. The preaching was not suitable, the preacher was not suitable, and his wife was not suitable; so you see they had an awful problem on their hands. With all of the trouble, the congregations were on the increase, offerings were good, many outsiders were standing by the truth, and souls were seeking God.

We were approaching the quarterly conference and things were tense, so I came to the conclusion that I had better send for my superior and have him present at that meeting. I told the officials that I had written for him but had received no reply. The night arrived, and I was totally in the dark; I did not know whether to expect him or not. When I entered the church several of the officials were there, "Well, is Rev. S—— coming?" they asked. I did not know so told them I did not . How innocent they acted! I learned later that they had been in a meeting with Brother S—— from about 6:00 to 7:00 o'clock that evening.

About 7:45 in came the Rev. ————. He spoke to everyone very cordially, then to me, took the chair and opened the meeting. The regular form of business was disposed of and then—"Well, now what is the difficulty here between preacher and people?" asked the Rev. S——. One by one the officials arose and displayed their "Old Man". including the big Mr.

J—— which was the worst. He arose and made a number of very kind remarks about himself, how he had given and stood by the church, etc., then how he dumped the garbage of his soul on us. Well, glory to God, no matter how much swill is poured on one from the sour soul of a carnal-hearted old professor, the honey of Heaven will keep him sweet. I tell you, if you want something scientific, that is, "something that is based on facts", as E. Stanley Jones puts it, move up to Pentecost and get your soul baptized with the Holy Ghost who has Perfect Love as one of His outstanding attributes. With all of these carnal bouquets lying at our feet we felt no spirit of retaliation within our hearts. Finally he left his beloved pastor, and went at his preaching. "Why don't he give us something interesting and good, instead of those bloody sermons?" he asked. "Blood, blood, blood is all we hear". When he spoke against the atonement, I felt the strength of Samson. At this there was a commotion through the congregation; the saints were sitting on the edges of their chairs expecting to see God do to him like He did to Ananias and Sapphira, while the other element were urging him on to say more.

When things quieted down and, after having a few remarks from the spiritual people, Brother S—— turned to where we were sitting. "Now, Brother Bradley, you have heard what has been said. These people are paying you and it behooves you to at least try to please them. What do you think about it?" I arose and felt like Paul as he testified before Felix. I stated that if I had been at all unkind in my deliverance of

the truth, I was sorry; but as for the truth that I
had preached, I believed it and would not recant; it
was Bible, our discipline supported it, and I intended
to continue preaching it. I said, "Mr. S——, I will
not cut the corners from the Word to please anyone."
Of all the amens! The air was full, the saints had on
their fighting togs and shields of faith to defend the
truth. It was an exciting time for a few minutes, but
through it all Perfect Love was our portion. I tell
you, my friend, it works. "Well," said Brother S——,
"I trust you can get together on this matter; how
many of you folks feel that you can endure Brother
Bradley until conference time, put up your hands?
All right, we are dismissed." Perhaps he thought it
was dismissed, but I believe there will be some that
will face that meeting at the great tribunal of the
skies for trampling the blood of the everlasting cove-
nant under their feet and counting it an unholy thing.
I let them endure me only one week and read my
resignation from the pulpit the following Sunday.

CHAPTER VI

A HOLINESS PREACHER WITHOUT A MOORING

We had intended to leave town after resigning, but a number of the members and friends desired us to stay and hold meeting in the house. This was all new to me but, being full of zeal for God and having an interest in some of the spiritual babies, we said that if God would open a way we would stay.

We had been renting our own apartment but the furniture all belonged to the church. If we stayed it meant that the Lord would undertake for us in furnishing our home, for we vowed that we would not go in debt for furniture.

I went to see Brother P—— who had held our revival meeting the winter before and told him how things had turned out. I told him I was waiting for the Lord to show me what to do.

In a few days he called me on the phone and said they had received a letter from his wife's mother saying that they were breaking up their home and would be glad to give them the furniture, providing they would come after it. Brother P—— said we were welcome to it as their parsonage was furnished, and that he had a truck he could borrow and we would drive to Jersey City and get it. We took this as a Divine opening and consented to the use of the furniture, drove to Jersey City and hauled it home.

Two days after we received the furniture the church sent a moving van and carted away all of their belongings, including dishes, pans, mops, etc. Well, God is never late but just on time, and that in providing every need, for along with the furniture had come dishes and everthing needful. Amen.

We commenced meeting in the living room on a warm Sunday night in early June, with a congregation of about twenty-five. We continued our services for three or four weeks and, of course, much to the displeasure of the other church; but God set His seal upon them. A certain doctor in town was very much interested in our stand for truth, having seen several accounts in the paper and heard many comments around town on the subject, both pro and con. Hearing of his interest and that he was quite a spiritual man, I determined to go and see him. I did, and we had a good chat together. He commended me on my stand and said he was interested in having a spiritual church in town. In a few days he came to see me and said the Lord had laid it on his heart that we should have a tent and wanted to know how much money we could raise toward it. I told him that there was no ready money available. However, he insisted that the Lord wanted a tent in the town.

In a few days he came back and took me to Philadelphia to a tent-maker's and inquired about prices. He was so positive that the Lord wanted a tent meeting; I presume finally the Spirit made it plain to him that he was the man to buy it. Well, he did, and made arrangement to have it shipped, and then secured a lot in a very desirable location of the town.

I felt there was something strange about the whole procedure but, having had no dealings with people of such type, I did not see through it as quickly as I might. After we had the tent and everything was moving, he began to deal with me about my personal experience, giving me tracts and Scripture on the gift of tongues. This perplexed me greatly and threw me into a quandary. The next thing, he was wanting to get me a good evangelist, namely, one from the Pentecostal movement.

Some of the people who were standing by the meetings, seeing that I had gotten on the fence, began to show a lack of interest. I was under the doctor's thumb, so to speak, and my people, who no doubt knew more about the Tongues Movement than I did, were leaving me, and I was on the fence as to my own experience. If there was a third definite experience I wanted it, for my heart was on a stretch after God. I knew that carnality was gone, but what about this tongues as the only evidence!

Well, I made up my mind that I would fight it out on my knees and on the authority of God's Word. I went at it and the Lord, praise His name, did not leave me alone. I sought earnestly for nearly a week and, little by little, the light began to break in as God opened the precious Word to me. I didn't ask the advice of others, but went directly to The Wonderful Counselor. Well, glory to God, He brought me out of the woods of perplexity and witnessed to my soul that the "Gift of Tongues" was not an evidence of the abiding Comforter, but rather a PURE HEART.

Amen! I have never been on the fence since over this question.

Taking my stand against the doctor's pet teaching did not set very well. It wasn't long until he began to press me for some money to pay for the tent.

The next thing was our getting in touch with a certain preacher who was in charge of a work in Philadelphia of an independent nature. We hadn't learned yet that some are wolves in sheep's clothing. We very cordially invited him to preach for us, and he did. What a peculiar slant he had on the Scriptures, and he did not hesitate about injecting it into his sermon that night, telling us emphatically that all who had a doctor would be lost. Well this was another blow to the little band, as again it threw them into a confusion, myself included. The older ones in the experience of Holiness went away wagging their heads, and stayed away, instead of taking us aside kindly and showing us the error on Scriptural foundation. Well, praise God for the Teacher Divine, the blessed Holy Ghost!

We managed, by the help of the Lord, to get out of the woods and underbrush of fanaticism again, but not without serious damage to the Christian experience of some, and I fear that they have never recovered from it. What a responsible position the man or woman has to whom God has entrusted the care of His little lambs. How I have looked back and wished that I had done differently. I was doing my best, however, so have had to plead the merits of the precious Blood for my ignorance, blunders and mistakes of those days.

We held forth in the tent all summer, but needless to say that with such a poor leader as they had in the person of myself, and the several blows from the powers of fanaticism, we hardly held our own. The attendance was fair, God helped in the preaching, and some sought and found both pardon and purity. With the doctor pressing us for money on the tent, some shaking their heads and saying we had gone off in fanaticism, and others on the fence as to their beliefs, it was a hard summer's fight.

In the fall, the Lord having stopped the supply of our needs and other things that evidenced our work was finished, we sold the tent and gave the doctor what it brought, said good-bye to the folks, packed up and left.

There certainly wasn't a great deal accomplished and one would almost question the Lord's will in the whole matter, but one thing that causes me to praise God for the summer's experience is that I settled some things regarding doctrinal questions that I never will forget, and, though without a mooring, denominationally, by the time the summer was ended I had my anchor with a firmer grip in the Rock of Ages, and was more fully grounded on the Immutable Word of God, which is a sure foundation when the winds of fanaticism and the storms of doubt are assailing one's spiritual building.

CHAPTER VII

FIRST EVANGELISTIC MEETINGS

I had decided definitely to go into the evangelistic field. After moving our things home with my people and having no responsibilities to hinder us, we were ready to launch out. The thing that confronted us was where we would launch first. I had never done evangelistic work before, and who would engage me?

Well, I sat down and wrote to all of my preacher friends and sent them an advertising card and then waited to see what would transpire. No doubt most of them had heard of the upheavel that had taken place during my last pastorate, and since most of my preacher friends at that time were more or less conservative, I do not wonder at them fearing to engage me.

In the meantime, the evangelist, Bro. E——, whom I had met in New York, began a meeting near our home. Of course, having received the blessed experience of Sanctification since we saw him last, we were more than anxious to see him and hear him preach. We attended regularly, and with a great deal of profit. At the close of his meeting he invited us to go with him in a meeting in South Jersey. We were delighted with the idea and, since I had not received any calls as yet myself, we felt it was providential. We had the Ford and he paid all of the expenses; so we were off.

Though we were absolutely penniless yet we were glad to be in the work (if it was playing "second fiddle"). We had a comfortable place to stay, congenial people, etc., but one day the general order of events was somewhat disturbed by a funeral at the dinner hour; so that instead of having three meals we had only two. After the service at night, we arrived home before the rest of the family and decided to walk down town and get a little fresh air. We had not walked far when we were aware of the fact that we were extremely hungry. We would not ask the people for something to eat; we were penniless and yet there was an awful gnawing in our stomachs. About the time we were feeling desperate for something to satisfy the awful craving, we arrived in front of a restaurant, or rather, a lunch room. We stopped. In the window were the largest, nicest frankfurters, or commonly speaking, "hot dogs" that I have ever seen. They were sizzling on a griddle and the fumes were being wafted out thru a ventilator above. I looked at wife and she at me, and then both of us looked at the "hot dogs". "Dear," she said, "don't you have even a dime so we can get one and break it in half?" Well, I had searched my pocket several times in the last few minutes, but went at it again, only to find it full of emptiness. We walked down the street a few blocks almost praying that we would find a piece of money. Finally we stopped in front of a bank window and got a good look at a dollar bill which was in the window in a frame. This climaxed all, so we turned and went back to the house, appetite and all, went to bed and forgot it.

In a few weeks we were with the same man in Delaware. Of course, when we were asked to go, we thought surely he would have us take some part in the services, especially the singing. Night after night we sat and listened and were not asked to do a thing. We were acquiring a great deal of knowledge by observation. Then, too, we were learning that grace could keep one blessed even though they were unnoticed. After the evangelist saw that we were patient and willing to be nothing, he asked us to sing a time or two. As I look back I wonder that he asked us at all. Though we had grown much in the year that we had known of Holiness, yet wife did not seem to grasp it and as a result she had a great deal of the worldly appearance clinging on.

Not long after we were married I had given her a fine string of pearls and she had continued wearing them up until a few months prior to this time. It seemed as though she couldn't keep them strung, for some reason or other. She did not know at that time. After a while she said she was going to take them to a jeweler and have them done right. In her mind she was saying: "Now if they do not hold together this time, I'll take it that it is wrong to wear them." We had heard no preaching along this line but God was leading us out. The thing that I cannot understand is how people can attend Holiness meetings right

along and never get light on such things. I have
come to the conclusion that they do not want to see it.
She had not had them from the jewelers more than a
few days when away they went in every direction,
and that was the end of the necklace.

While in this meeting I had a peculiar experience.
We had been acquainted with a young man who had
gone to Chicago to prepare for the Lord's work. One
night I dreamed that he was about to be married and
was getting into a terrible trap, having been deceived
by a girl who was a professing Christian and the
daughter of a missionary. I awoke so depressed that
I could hardly bear it. And how the spirit of prayer
came upon me! I felt greatly relieved and went back
to sleep. In the morning the dream was so upon
my mind that I felt I should write him, warning him
to be careful. I wrote just as I had dreamed and,
in a few days, to my surprise I received a letter from
him asking me who had been writing about his affair,
and went on to state that I had the case just as it
was and that God answered prayer and delivered him
from the snare.

Before the meeting in Delaware closed we received
a telegram from home that my brother Wesley was
sick in the hospital. We packed up and left immediately.

The summer before this we had been greatly concerned about his soul's salvation. We knew that he
was going with a group of young folks who were rated
among the "uppers", traveling to dances, dinner par-
ties, etc. He and another lad were on their way home

one night, or rather, it was early one Sunday morning, from some pursuit of pleasure they had been following. Wesley was at the wheel, though the car belonged to the other fellow who was asleep by his side. They were within fifteen miles of home when Wesley fell asleep, too. He awoke with a start and just as he opened his eyes he saw that they were about to crash into a parked car. In an instant it was all over. He was hurled through the curtain to the side of the road, while both cars were enveloped in flames. Not losing consciousness, he immediately thought of his chum, ran to the car and in the midst of the flames pulled the door open, reached in and dragged the unconscious form to safety, beating out the flames on his clothing.

Dear grandmother, gone to heaven since then, said that she could not sleep all night but prayed that God would spare Wesley from the awful danger that seemed to hang over him. He came in limping in the morning, cut and bruised and badly shaken up, but not seriously hurt. This circumstance had driven us to our knees more than anything else. I remember so vividly praying that God would save his soul if it was necessary to bring him to death's door. Well, little did we know that He had commenced to answer our prayers.

We arrived home to find that his condition was not so grave as we expected. We found him nearly covered with eczema, but not seriously ill. We visited him at the hospital, but did not see any marks of repentance; however, we kept holding him up in prayer.

Before we had time to go back to Delaware for the closing of the meeting, we received a letter from a young preacher by the name of W—— in West Virginia, saying that he would use me for a meeting. We had gone to seminary together and were well acquainted, so that I looked forward to a good time.

My brother gave us some money for which we were very thankful and set out for West Virginia early one morning in November. We drove all day and late into the night, had several flat tires and went the last few miles on the rim, but we arrived though weary and tired. We got W—— out of bed to let us in, but to our surprise we received a very cool reception. In the morning we noticed he was a little more natural and finally expressed himself as not having expected us to come so soon.

We were not long noticing that W——'s spiritual life was at a very low ebb. After a few days, the meetings were arranged for on one point of the circuit, which happened to be in a small mining town between two mountains

Monday night was the first service, and W—— and I went alone, leaving Sister Bradley at home with his sister who was keeping house for him. We arrived after traveling about nine miles over a rough mountain road. It was a dirty, dingy, little mining town, with peculiar little houses and a lot of black fences. When we arrived at the church, to my surprise and regret, they had oil lamps and few of them too, and I had notes to preach by or could not preach.

Well, the service began and finally I got to preaching but with great difficulty in reading my notes. However, with all my handicaps and embarrassments, God was working, for when I finished Bro. W—— jumped to his feet and said, "The devil is in this place tonight and, furthermore, he is in me. I am going to pray for you and I want you to pray for me. Let us rise and be dismissed."

This nearly took me off my feet. I had been praying for a good meeting but hardly thought it would begin in such a manner. On the way home he told me that he was not feeling right in his soul, said he had slipped away quite a little.

The next morning I heard him up bright and early talking with his sister, who was a nurse. When we arose I learned that he had been talking over his condition with her and they had decided that it was a physical depression instead of spiritual. I did n't say much but was thinking a great deal, and wife and I discussed it between us.

Having had so much trouble with my notes the first night, I had prayed it thru and told the Lord that if He would help me I would scrap them and trust Him. I have been doing it ever since and He has never let me down once, but has, as promised, "brought all things to my remembrance." I must give Him all the praise, for ordinarily I have a poor memory.

On Tuesday night Bro. W—— did not go to the
service as he had a meeting at one of the other appointments. He had only five. When we returned
from service he was home and told me how much the
Lord had blessed him in preaching that night. I told
him I was glad and said no more.

The next night, Wednesday, he did not go again,
having another appointment to fill. When wife and
I returned he had another good report of how the
Lord had blessed him. I told him again that I was
glad and said no more.

Thursday night he and his sister, wife, and I all
went, but Bro. W—— said he was not feeling very
well and asked me if I would go on with the service
and he would sit in the pew with the folks. Well, I
was glad to have him before me rather than behind,
for I had a strange feeling that something was about
to take place. I do not remember the text, but the
Lord was wonderfully helping when instantly there
came to my mind an occurrence that had taken place
in W——'s life, and it had never been straightened
up. He did not know that I knew it and I had forgotten it entirely until the Spirit brought it to my
remembrance. It had happened two or three years before. It was an apt illustration for the closing of
the message and I gave it out as the Lord brought it
to mind. As I told it, I saw him begin to change
color, and then his position; next he looked to see
how many were watching him, supposing that every
one knew who I was speaking of, though I had not
inferred that it was he. There was no move toward

an altar service, so I dismissed, with W—— gripping the pew and white as death.

He has told me since that if he had had a revolver he would have blown my brains out as I stood behind the desk. He said, "Floyd, there was murder in my heart and I would have put it into action had I been in possession of a weapon."

By the time we reached home, his awful anger had abated greatly and after the others had retired, he said, "Well, God has found me, Old Man", and then proceeded to confess his true state, the restitution that he would have to make to the people on the charge and what it would mean to pay the price and to tell them he had been backslidden ever since he had been pastor there. I talked with him and prayed with him but to no avail. He said it was no use, that he had played with God's mercy too long and there was no help for him. What a picture! How he paced the floor, pulled his hair and groaned, but could not shed a tear!

On Friday and Saturday his condition was really alarming. God showed him it was something more than general debility. I wondered if he would commit suicide rather than face the thing thru. Saturday night he told me that if he felt the Spirit striving with him in the least he would head for the altar, no matter where or when.

He had asked me to preach at the Sunday morning appointment and he took no part in the service at all. While I was doing my best and under the anointing of the Spirit, I noticed that he was wiping the tears. I made a brief ending and gave the altar call. In an instant he was on his feet and at the altar, but when he struck the mercy bench the tears dried and he was as hard as adamant. There were several seeking and when they were finished he stood to his feet, faced the congregation and told them frankly that they had a backslidden preacher; that he had played the hypocrite ever since he had been their pastor and that wherein he had wronged any of them he would be around just as fast as he could to make things right. He told them further that his heart was as hard as stone; that he was a lost, un-done soul and that if God did not come to his help he would never stand behind the desk again. He closed with the statement that he would be at the church Monday night for a meeting and would have the victory or his resignation.

I am satisfied that if we had more honesty such as this in the pulpit, we would have more converts in the pew.

In the afternoon I filled his appointment and then went to O—— for the revival service at night. He had an evening service himself, and having no one to send, was compelled to go so as not to disappoint the people. He told his sister that the only thing he could do was to go and tell the members just what he had confessed in the morning. He had no message, nor experience.

He said that as they drove to D—— that night in the old buggy, with the rain pattering on the roof, he, with a heavy heart, a wrecked ministry, and a blank outlook for the future, his sister began singing:

"Simply trusting every day,
Trusting thru a stormy way
Even when my faith is small,
Trusting Jesus, that is all."

As he joined her with the tenor the words burned into his heart— faith gripped the promise, he trusted and the burden rolled away. The light of heaven seemed to illuminate the old buggy, and the victory was in his heart.

They drove on to the church, singing, shouting and crying. Upon his arrival he went into the pulpit like a storm; he did not preach but merely told them of his experience, gave the altar call and had the first soul during his ministry.

Needless to say he was at the church the next night, but not with his resignation. He had been on the go the greater part of the day, making restitution and talking with people about their souls' salvation, and came to the service like a whirlwind. He could not stand to see any one out of the ark of safety but was button-holing every one in town. Some of the folks thought that he had suddenly become demented. But it was not head trouble, it was heart trouble of a very desirable kind.

The revival was on. The altar was lined with seekers night after night, and preacher, people and evangelist were going up country.

A few months later we returned and held a meeting on another point of the circuit and with wonderful success. The folks came night after night, filling the church to its capacity and lining the altar with the penitents. Young men and women were converted, old women threw away their snuff boxes, immorality was uncovered, and the town and preacher were on fire for God, while many of the old hardshells found fault and criticised.

CHAPTER VIII

A HOME TRANSFORMED

While we were in meetings with W—— in W. Va., we received a letter from home stating that Father and Brother had been converted, and the latter had been raised from a deathbed. Well, we laughed and shouted and glorified God for answered prayer.

My brother had stayed in the hospital for about five weeks; all kinds of tests had been made to determine the cause of his condition, but with no avail. He, of course, had made his boast that he was going to get cured of that annoying disease, but God had shown him differently. He paid his bill of several hundred dollars and was discharged, having been told they could do nothing for him.

He came home very much dejected. Serious thoughts were running through his mind, though he said nothing to anyone about it. After he had been a few days at home, continually getting worse, he asked Mother and Grandma if they would not remember him in prayer. They were very much surprised and though they were only nominal Christians they remembered him before the throne from time to time. The days wore on but there was no improvement, and they noticed that his head and neck, which were covered with eczema, began to swell.

After suffering dreadfully all day with an increased swelling, his head was the size of a bucket by night.

When Father came home he saw that his condition was serious and insisted on calling a doctor, being satisfied that erysipelas had set in. My brother with head and face laid open in great gashes told them emphatically that he was through with the doctors, that he had given himself to the Lord, and if He did not heal him, he was all ready to go. This was like fanaticism to my father, but my brother insisted that it was so and refused to have a doctor.

Father was crushed. We were three hundred miles from home and the only other child in a dying condition. At last, very late, they retired, but not to sleep. After much rolling and tossing Father began to cry right out for the Lord to help them. Mother said, "N——, let us get out of bed and pray right." He said he did not know how to pray, but after a little he assented and they knelt down together for the first time since they had been married—nearly twenty-five years.

Such crying and praying as he did, and Mother too. All the while he was asking the Lord to spare their son, but received no help from on high. Father says that after awhile he realized that he was on the wrong track and began to tell the Lord that he was in need himself; told Him that He could have all he possessed, and that he would serve Him if He would only spare the boy. Still no help came. Then in desperation he said, "Lord, if you want to take him, he is ready. I am willing, and I will serve Thee anyway". Almost instantly the burden rolled away and, with a deep settled peace he got into bed and slept like a baby until morning.

It was Thanksgiving Day and, after such an experience the night before, Father felt as though he wanted someone around that could really pray, so he drove sixty miles and brought a great Aunt home with him, full of faith in Jesus. Wesley was about the same when they returned, so she went right to his room and began to find out where he stood spiritually. After a long talk she said, "Wesley, I believe that the Lord can heal you". The strong assertion of her faith was like a life line to a drowning man, and he grasped it. They bundled him up in blankets, put him in the car and drove about ten miles to a preacher that believed in healing and would anoint him according to James 5:14. When he returned, he was able to sit at the table and eat his supper. This was on Thursday night. On Friday he was well enough and the swelling was gone so that he could put on a collar and go to Philadelphia to see his friend.

When we returned home after a long cold trip, many flat tires, and a leaky radiator, we found enough to make our hearts leap for joy. We found Mother and Grandma had gotten a new grip on God; Father was a new man and Brother had been transformed. "Praise God from whom all blessings flow!" He had not only answered prayer for one but had brought the entire family into the fold.

There was no mistake but that a great change had taken place in Father for he was talking religion all the time and of how good God had been to him. However, I noticed that he was still tasting of the filthy weed occasionally. Though he seemed happy and had no trouble to express himself, yet when we went to prayer as a family he did not seem to be able to get his mouth open. He lamented the fact greatly but said that he just could not do it. Well, there was a reason for we learned that the Spirit had been talking to him about the tobacco.

One afternoon Brother was not so well, and we all went to his room to have prayer with him. Several of us prayed, but there did not seem to be any answer. Finally, he began to break loose and he told the Lord that he would give up the unsaved girl he was going with. It really seemed as though he would die. This made a great impression upon Father and naturally he felt as though he wanted to help pray, too. We had all prayed until we were hoarse. Brother was still under that awful pressure, and Father could not seem to open his mouth. In a little while I heard a great commotion and looked up in time to see him jump to his feet and in desperation run his hand first in one pocket and then the other. I saw in an instant what was up and began to shout the victory. He was gathering all of the scraps of tobacco and pieces of cigars together and then like a pitcher on a ball field he wound up and fired it into the waste basket with a "bang'. Then he dropped on his knees and went to praying with all his might. Well, glory to God, the longer he prayed the more the blessing fell until we were all laughing and shouting and praising God! Brother's burden was gone, and we were all on the mountain top. By and by Father got on his feet and, with tears running and face shining, he staggered up against the wall like a drunken man, intoxicated with the power of presence of God.

It was about four-thirty when we began to pray, and when the glory abated so that we could be ourselves it was nearly eight o'clock. Father had used tobacco about forty years, but God delivered him from the appetite in less than forty seconds. Amen!

Wesley gave up his unsaved girl friend, and in a few weeks the Lord saved her, turned her into a real old shouting Methodist and gave her back to him. Now they are husband and wife.

Several weeks later the Spirit spoke to Father about giving a tenth of his income. He was so elated over all that had taken place that he yielded gladly. In a few days the Lord asked him if he did not think he ought to give a tithe of the past year's salary. Well, this was a little different, but like a blessed person he assented. After the Lord received the consent of his will, He said, "Now there is your boy traveling around the country in that old broken-down Ford, why not use that tithe money and get him a new car?" When he broke the news to us that we should run the old car to the garage and get a new one and he would pay the bill, it almost seemed like a dream. We did it without any hesitation. Praise the Lord!

After returning from a meeting we learned that they were having revival services in a certain church and, being anxious to get Father into the experience of Sanctification, we arranged for all of the family to attend. After several nights of red-hot truth, we noticed that Father did not seem to be warming up to the teaching of a second work of grace.

We returned from service one night and, as was quite customary, had a little lunch before we went to bed. We were nearly finished when the conversation ran into a discussion about the preaching. Father said, "Well, nobody can live the Bible anyway". The statement crushed me, for I knew that a little of such an attitude would mean death to what grace he had enjoyed. The Spirit fell on me, and I sprang to my feet and began to praise God for the blessed Holy Ghost, the experience of Sanctification, the destruction of the carnal mind. I had spoken only a few words when I fell prostrate on the floor under the power of the Spirit. Wife said that immediately the folks thought that I was dead. I was, but to sin. Surely the experience that I had been in possession of by faith had been changed to feeling. Wife understood, for we had seen such before, and she would not let them touch me. Praise God, He will vindicate Himself and His sacred Word of truth. After nearly three hours my strength returned, and we retired.

The next day it seemed as though we were moving in a different sphere. The very house seemed sacred. The folks moved around on tiptoe and spoke in whispers.

The taking of my stand against Father had brought about an estrangment; when he came home in the afternoon I was in my room praying so that we did not see each other. Wife sat down to the piano and began to play some of the old hymns and after several she noticed that Father had his head in his hands and was weeping. She went to him and said, "Papa, let's go up and have Floyd pray with us". They arose and started. About this time I was strongly impressed to go downstairs and I started also. We met on the

landing and fell into each others arms and then to our
knees. What a time of praying! In a little while my
brother and his friend came and they joined in. When
we were through, Father knew something about the
demonstration of the Spirit and has always believed
in Holiness from then on.

What a change in our home! How many seasons of
fellowship and prayer around the family altar, times
when the blessing would be so great that the air
seemed to be impregnated with Divine power. Such
times will linger in our memory while the ages roll.

CHAPTER IX

INTO A SWEET BUSINESS

I had just returned from some meetings in Pennsylvania where I had been assisting a preacher as his singer. The place had been as barren as the land of Lodebar. Money was scarce, and some debts that had been incurred in the tent meetings of the summer before were staring me in the face. What could I do to make some money and liquidate my obligations? My wife had been working and that had helped, but it seemed that I was not doing a thing. As I see it now I wasn't even trusting. It is a whole lot easier to kick over the traces, run ahead of God and get into trouble than it is to "stand still and see the salvation of the Lord."

"Well Dear," Wife said, "I have a wonderful proposition for you. I believe we can get out of debt by September, and then we will be free to go into the work without any handicap." "Fine, well now tell me all about it." So Wife and I sat down together and she told me the whole story: Two of my preacher friends were going into the candy business and I was to be a third party, to go on the road and sell. The machinery was all bought, a place had been rented and everything was ready for operation the coming Monday. They were to specialize in molasses pop corn rolls, and later on to work in some other line of confections. There was not a question but what

103

I could make between forty and fifty dollars a week. My, what a salary for a Holiness preacher that needed money! I thought this was the most fascinating word picture that had ever come to my attention and, of course, like the fish after the bait, I bit, and swallowed the hook and all.

It was no doubt a good business, profitable and legitimate, but not for three preachers. The only business for the man or woman who is called of God to the sacred work, is the business of getting people sweetened up for heaven, and that not in their stomachs but in their souls. Amen!

Monday morning I was on the job with the rest, bright and early. What a fine place, right on the main street! The help was all there and three preachers. We donned our white aprons, rolled up our sleeves and commenced action. The first thing was for all to turn in, learn how to operate the machinery and get out a good batch of candy, so that the salesman could go on the road. It was the month of June, a sultry day, and the heat from the vat of boiling molasses and pop corn poppers only assisted the mercury to run higher. We turned out our batch and the girls went to wrapping. It looked like a real factory. Several passers-by stopped at the window to watch, and it seemed as though the town was interested in our success. But I have learned, as some one has said, "It isn't the spurt at the start that counts, but the steady going."

The other preachers having steady work, one as a pastor, the other as an evangelist, naturally their time was somewhat divided. Along about the end of the first week one went away in meetings, to be gone about a month. As I had some work inside as well as being on the road, I felt it necessary to live near, and so rented a cottage in the camp meeting grove at the edge of the town and moved, bag and baggage. You see I was depending on the spurt instead of the steady going. Well, the spurt did not last long. We seemed to be selling, but yet did not have enough to pay our help and meet the bills, too. My father, who was in-terested in my financial affairs and wanted to help me get on top, put some money into the business at this juncture, to save the day. And still things did not look encouraging. About this time I noticed that Bro. C—— was growing faint hearted. I confess I had started to wilt some myself. One morning he came in late and said, "Well, Bro. B——, the Lord never called me to make pop corn candy but to preach the Gospel; I'm through, you can go on with it if you want to." Well, well, another stockholder with-drawing. Wife and myself and one or two girls that were still with us decided we would make the best of it. We made it, we ate it, we sold it, we dreamed about it. Yes, I mean *Molasses Pop Corn Candy*. It seemed as though every time we turned around some one had left the plug out of the molasses barrel and there was a puddle of profits to clean up. It was a sweet business. We had a job to keep the flies away. Everything was sweet and sticky, and everybody had the blues.

At last we found it necessary to move to smaller quarters, and now there was no one but U. S. & Co. (Wife and I). Many a night we would work until

twelve and later getting ready to go on the road the
next day. How we would boil molasses candy and
mix pop corn, wondering how we could stand it another hour; get up in the morning with only a few
hours' rest and start on the road and then find no sale
for the goods. And with all of these business de-
pressions and financial handicaps, we were thinking
What if Jesus should come and we be found running
like a mad man to sell some one a roll of pop corn!
What a condition! Sometimes we drove for miles
and did not realize it. After such a precious experience, such a positive call to the work of the Gospel
and then to get tied up in such a way! I did not
blame any one. They were all trying to help me, but
in trying to help me out they helped me further in.

In making my rounds one day, tired, weary and discouraged, I stopped at a certain camp meeting to see
some one. While there I met an official of the camp.
We passed the time of day and he inquired as to how
the pop corn business was going. Well, that was
enough for me. I told him not well and began to un-
load my heart and tell him how God was bringing me
to time, and that I felt I should be preaching instead
of wasting my time. I was hoping for a word of
encouragement; I was asking for bread, but to my
surprise I received a stone. He shoved his hands into
his pockets, looked at me through squinted eyes and
said, "Perhaps you are like a lot of other exhausters
running around the country." Is that all the help one
could expect from a Christian man of mature years?
I left the camp hurriedly, got into my car and started
for home, heart sick, condemned and crushed. Before

I reached home I had gotten myself together somewhat
and determined that I would preach no matter what
he or any one else thought of me. But what about
Father? What about his money? I could not throw
up the business until I had paid him back at least.
What about the machinery belonging to Bro.E——?
What about the bills I had created since I had been
in the thing? Oh, my, what could I do? I was tied
hand and foot; there was no way out. May God keep
every preacher that reads this from ever getting into
such a dilemma as I was in. It is easier to get out of
the will of God than to get back in it. Well, apparently there was nothing to do but settle down and
try to make a success of it.

It was approaching the Fourth of July. Surely if
ever the business would go over the top it would now.
My wife and I worked like slaves. We filled what few
cans we had in and then packed it in cartons. Monday, Tuesday and Wednesday were to be big days, as
the Fourth fell on Thursday. I do not remember how
much stock we had on hand, but enough to put us on
top financially. Monday was quite a fair day but during the night it began to rain. It rained all night and
all day Tuesday. I went on the road and disposed of
some of the goods, selling that in the cans first and
then that in the cartons. While I was making quite
a deal with a certain storekeeper, he questioned as to
the freshness of the candy. "Oh yes," said I and un-
wrapped some for him to try, and to my surprise it
was soft and stale looking. I plundered every carton
only to find that the dampness had ruined it all, and
me along with it. This seemed like a climax to the

whole affair. I went home and there we sat, Wife and I, bemoaning our awful state. Next morning we arose, went to the shop to make up more. But what was the use? All the cans were out, there was nothing but cartons to put it in, and it was still raining. We sat around, talked, cleaned up a little and finally went back to the cottage. While lunch was in preparation I mused over the situation. We took our places at the table but not to eat. I was at the fork of the road; something had to be done and that immediately. I pushed my plate back. My dear companion spoke a few kind words and I broke. Down on my knees I went, and she by my side. Such praying! Piece by piece I replaced my consecration on the altar, told God I was done with the pop corn business and that from then on I would preach. I remember telling Him that if I could not get a church to preach in, I would preach on a soap box. Praise God! when I got to this juncture the fire fell and pop corn balls went a-flying. Molasses sweetness had no comparison with what filled my soul that Wednesday noon in that little old cottage. How we shouted and cried and laughed! Well, we felt richer by far than a millionaire. Amen! While in the state of extreme ecstasy, the Lord brought to our mind a little village in the Catskills and made it clear that our first meeting was to be held there.

I did my best to get some one to take over the business and began to make arrangement to leave for New York State. I did not know how Father would take it when he found it out, nor how Bro. E—— would feel at my leaving in such haste; but God had put the

Divine urge in my soul and I could do nothing but move. It did not take long for Sunday to arrive; in the midst of packing, teaching some one else the formula for the pop corn candy and other minor arrangements, the time slipped by rapidly. My only fear was, What will Father say? I knew he would be at church Sunday night and when I thought about it my heart would sink with despair. But with it all I was determined to do the will of God no matter what any one thought. Glory to God! I am glad He can give us a backbone like steel.

It was service time. We went and who should be there but Father. The pastor had asked me to preach, and I did and made some firm declarations. I think Father surmised something and when the service was out he said he would come over a while. I knew what was coming; he would wonder why we were all packed and no doubt would do some questioning. He and the folks came in. I could see that he was looking closely. Everything was bare and we were ready to move in the morning. We talked and talked; the conversation was strained and so was I. It did not seem as though I could muster enough courage to speak my convictions. They arose to go and still nothing was said; we went out to the car and they got in.

The grove was in puddles. The trees were dripping, as it had poured rain for about two hours and had just stopped. How would I get at it, especially at such a late hour and the folks about ready to go? Finally the spell was broken: "What are you intending to do?" he asked. I told him God had called me to preach and I would have to do it; I had gotten into an awful predicament; I was sorry and intended to pull up stakes and go. "Where are you going?" he asked. I explained that I was going to New York state for a meeting. "Did I have a call?" No. "To what church was I going?" I didn't know. How ridiculous it all sounded. I do not blame him for thinking so, but through it all I knew what God wanted me to do and I intended doing it. "What about the business?" came the pointed question, and then a good lecturing.

Let me say here that no matter what degree of grace we may enjoy, it is impossible for us to know God's dealings with others. Each must fight the thing through for himself. I did not blame Father. He saw it alone from is own point of view.

Here I will insert part of a letter describing the experience that followed. The letter was written by my wife to a friend, a few days after the occurrence:

"July 30, 1926.

"My Dear Mable:

"The story about our short stay in Pitman is a long one, however, I will endeavor to tell a little of how we happened to go there and how God, for Jesus' sake, delivered us from the snare Satan had planned for us.

"Early last spring when Floyd returned from Indiana, Pa., where he had been in meetings, a friend of ours was opening a candy pop corn business in Pitman. He offered us both work at a good salary; and, since we had no meetings booked ahead, and the way seemingly did not open for any, we talked it over and decided this would be a wonderful way for us to spend the summer. We thought we would get some old debts that had been hanging on a long while paid off and be ready in the fall to again enter the fields which were already white unto harvest.

"We rented a cottage in the Old Pitman Camp Meeting grove and started to work making pop corn balls. Everything seemed to be going fine for about the first three weeks when I began to notice a decided change in Floyd. I did not mention it to him until two weeks ago on Wednesday. I had left the store early and gone over to the cottage to prepare lunch. About 12:30 Floyd came in, sad and dejected looking. We sat down to the table, but not to eat. We were about ready to return thanks when Floyd pushed his plate back and said, 'I can't eat.' Although I knew, I said, 'Why dear, what is the trouble?' At that he fell from his chair to the floor and began to pray as I have never heard him pray before. He prayed, he cried, he groaned. Oh, how my heart ached for him as he told God how he had been a disobedient servant and pleaded that if He would only return unto him the joy of his salvation, he would preach if it was from a soap box on a street corner. What a prayer meeting we had!

"We both realized we were out of Divine order and thus we were drifting away from Him who loved us and gave Himself for us. We had been so busy that we had failed to take time for prayer and Bible study. Oh yes, we had our family altar, prayed a few minutes every night and morning, but had neglected the secret place of prayer and tarrying before Him, and

this means sure defeat to any soul. When one neg-
lects this we may look for defeat and failure, for we
dare not walk alone.

"We prayed and cried for about an hour. When
we rose from our knees he said to me: 'I'm going to
preach Jesus and Him crucified, whatever the cost
may be.' I said 'Amen' to it all and told him I was
willing to do whatever he felt God would have us do,
and if I had in any way been the means of him getting out of Divine order I wanted him to forgive me.
My, what a happy time we had for another hour
praising God and renewing broken vows.

"Our rent was paid up until Monday, so we decided
to use the next three days packing our things and getting ready to leave the first of the week for any field
of labor the Lord might open for us. Floyd's folks
came down for church on Sunday night and the problem that faced us now was what Papa would say about
us leaving so unexpectedly after he had invested some
money in the business to help get it started.

"After service they went over to the cottage with
us and they could see we were all torn up to move;
but nothing was said about the business except that
it was not going so very well, until they were leaving.

"When they were ready to leave we went out to the
car to bid them good-bye. Floyd stood on the driver's
side, as Papa was at the wheel. I stood on the other
side talking with Mother, Ella and Wesley were in
the back seat.

"Papa asked Floyd what he intended to do. He said
he intended leaving within the next few days for

Preston Hollow, New York, which he felt God had laid on his heart. Papa said, 'What about the business?' Floyd told him he was leaving it in the care of Bro. S——, a friend of ours who has a butter and egg business, and that he was going to work the two together.

"Then papa asked him if he had been called to Preston Hollow, and he said, "No,' only he felt God leading him there. Papa had been saved only a few months and of course he could not understand the Spirit leading us thus. We hardly understood it ourselves, but we were glad to feel He was opening a door for us. I believe we know a little now of how Jonah felt when he got out of the whale's belly, glad to go if only the way were opened. Papa spoke rather sharply to Floyd, rebuking him for such a ridiculous idea of going to a place without being called by a church or a pastor. He had no sooner finished speaking than Floyd threw up both hands and cried out: 'O Jesus!' and fell to the ground as though he had been struck by lightning and lay there as if he were dead. We all ran to him screaming and crying and Wesley fell across him and began to pray and cry for God to spare his life. We all thought at first that he was dead, but after what I had seen on Wednesday I felt this was the Holy Ghost witnessing to him that he was in Divine order.

"Folks in the grove heard us crying and praying and as it was very late they gathered from every direction clad in pajamas, kimonos and bath robes, all inquiring what the trouble was with him. Some said he had a stroke, some said he had been run over by a car, others said he fainted, while others believed he was dead. When they learned I was his wife they all pitied me and offered their services to take him to a hospital, or get a doctor or whatever I wanted them to do. I thanked them and said that I did not want anything, that he was being blessed by the Holy Ghost and I did not want him disturbed. They turned on me instantly and said I was crazy and ought to be arrested. My, what an angry mob of people!

"He lay on his back, his body rigid, and he twisted and twisted for about twenty minutes. Then his body began to rise until it was bow shaped with only his feet and head touching the ground. Then he rolled on his stomach and it really looked as though his heels and head would meet.

"The crowd by this time were in a fury, so Papa said we had better take him into the house, and they picked him up and carried him in and laid him on the kitchen floor.

"His body by this time was not so rigid. He lay there as though he were in great agony and he began to make a very queer noise. I got down on my knees beside him and whispered in his ear. I said: "If you hear me, Darling, I want you to say Yes to Jesus, Whatever He wants us to do, we'll go through together. I'll stand by you, and we'll preach the Gospel and go anywhere He wants us to go?

"I had no sooner finished speaking to him than he gave a scream and jumped to his feet, began to roll up his sleeves and ran out of the house, screaming at the top of his voice: "Jesus is coming!! Prepare to meet God!!!" This he repeated over and over, running from house to house, warning people and preaching as he went, and Wesley and I after him. Wesley was saying, "Preach it, Floyd, preach it; I'll stand by you!"

"Folks thought he had gone crazy; his hair was almost standing up; his shirt was open at the neck as they had taken his collar off, and now he had rolled his sleeves half-way up his arms. Well, some ran from him, others ran toward him.

"One man came toward him with his fist drawn and said, 'If you don't shut up I'll smash your face.' Wesley said, 'No you won't either. He's my brother and you're going to let him alone.'

"Floyd paid no attention to any of these things; he went right on preaching, warning men to flee from the wrath to come. I can't tell you what he said. I was busy keeping the crowd away from him. He preached so fast and so loud, I wonder how he ever got his breath.

"Well, just as this moment I looked up and here came two armed officers, a big one and a little one. The big one grabbed hold of Floyd's arm, and when he did I grabbed him and said, 'Brother, this man is filled with the Holy Ghost, you had better not put your hands on him.' He said, 'Well the Holy Ghost can't keep the whole neighborhood up all night.' I said, 'He can if He want to, and you had better not touch him or you may drop dead.' I asked him if he would want to hinder the Holy Ghost, and he said,

"No", but that he would have to do something as the people were complaining. He said, 'Let me take him down to the station until he gets quiet.' I said, 'No, God has given him a message for his people and he's got to give it to them.'

"Then some one suggested that they go and get Brother Sturgis, pastor of the little Holiness church that we had been attending. So they sent the little officer after him while the big one stayed there to guard.

"Brother Sturgis told us afterwards that he heard this wild rap at the door and when he opened it there stood the most frightened cop he ever saw. He said, 'Mr. Sturgis, come quick, there's a man down here in the grove filled with the Holy Ghost.'

"In a few minutes here came Brother Sturgis and the little frightened cop behind him. He asked me what the trouble was and I told him as best I could in a few words. He saw there was no use trying to stop him, so he suggested singing him down. He started singing 'There is a Fountain Filled with Blood.' Floyd took up the thought and said: 'Yes, there is a fountain filled with blood, set up in the house of David for sin and uncleanness,' and on he went preaching, preaching, preaching. Stop him, why you couldn't stop him; you couldn't stand it to touch him, there was so much of the Holy Ghost power in him. He preached on until 1:30 in the morning; then we got him back into the house. He was still preaching, but not so fast nor so loud. He was in the house only a few minutes when he fell into a chair exhausted. He sat there praising God for another half hour, then we asked him if he would lie down and rest. He did not resist, so we led him to the couch and laid him down. How I wish you could have seen him, he lay there with his hands folded across his breast and a smile on his face like I have never seen in all my life and from his face beamed a light that every one could see, saint and sinner. He was lying in a dark room and what a holy, hallowed presence settled upon every one. I shall never forget it, nor will any one else who saw it.

"He spent the rest of the night praising God in a low undertone of voice, not sleeping any until about five o'clock in the morning.

"Later that day we moved our things to Mother's and left on Wednesday morning for Preston Hollow, New York. When we arrived, Floyd went to the Methodist preacher and told him how God had laid it on his heart to come there and hold a revival. He said that he and his people had been praying for God to send them a man for their revival and here he was. 'We began services last Sunday night. The crowds are good, and there have been several hands for prayer, I believe God is going to give us a good meeting in this place.'

"They tell us that the next evening the paper stated there were from eight hundred to a thousand people crowded in the grove to see a man filled with the Holy Ghost, and the caretaker there said: 'What about the time when five hundred lay as dead men in that same grove during the days of Pitman and Inskip? Now when one man gets the Holy Ghost it stirs the whole town.'

"The prayer of my heart is that God will ever keep us yielded vessels, meet for the Master's use."

*   *   *   *   *   *   *

All that I feel to say about the experience is that it was the most wonderful I have ever had. It was so sacred that words mean little in describing it. It seemed like Divinity had taken complete possession of the temple of clay. The prayer of my heart is that God will ever keep me true. What an awful thing it would be to cool off after enjoying such manifestations of the Holy Ghost!"

CHAPTER X

ON THE ROAD FOR GOD

After arranging all of our affairs we were on our road to New York state and had a singer with us. It was a step of faith, but I was so sure that God was directing that nothing could stop my purpose to do His will.

We stopped with some friends about fifteen miles from the village that God had laid on my heart. The next day I set out to look the ground over. There were two churches, a Baptist and a Methodist; I felt impressed to go to the Methodist pastor and see what could be arranged.

I hunted the parsonage with the determination that I would carry out the leading of the Spirit and hold a meeting in the town, if I had to stand on a soap box to do it. I was soon introducing myself to the preacher, whom I found to be rather a young man and very agreeable. I told him how the Lord had laid the place on my heart, and that I would like to have the use of the church, without obligating the members for one penny; and, of course, any results that might be derived, I would use my influence to turn them his way. As I spoke, I noticed his face lit up. Then he said that he had been praying that the Lord would send something to stir the community. Well, Amen! It looked like it was the something. He said he would speak to the Board about it and let me know.

In a day or so he came and told me that it was all right, but that every one felt that it was a bad time of the year. The farmers in the neighborhood were in the midst of haying and, then too, things were bad financially, but I was welcome to try it if I wanted, as long as the church was under no obligation financially.

Well, I told him I was willing for I wanted to obey God and not get swallowed by some whale. It was not any trying, as far as I was concerned, for I knew that the Lord of hosts had sent me, came with me, and had promised never to leave me. I took the last three dollars I had and left an order for the printing of some posters.

We arrived at the church Sunday night and to our surprise, and the surprise of all, the cars were parked in thick and the church, seating perhaps two hundred, well filled. The meeting ran for two weeks with such a congregation nearly every night and the church filled to its capacity on Sundays. The Lord gave us a good hearing, a good meeting, and an offering of about a hundred dollars without doing more than passing the basket. Praise God, He certainly did reward my faith and give me a determination to never get tied up in pop-corn or anything else, but to go north, east, south, and west preaching the Gospel as He had called me to do. And I have been at it ever since with more work than I could take care of.

I visited a man in the hospital a few months ago
that had received help in that meeting. The first
thing he said when he recognized me was, "I am still
enjoying that pure Love that you taught us about."

We left for New Jersey at the close of the meetings
but did not know where we were going next. We
did not have one call; but after the way God had
proven Himself, we were confident that something
would open up.

Two days after we arrived home we had a telegram
from a camp in Maryland saying that they would like
to have us come if we were free. Something had happened that they were disappointed in their man and
had thought of us. By the next Sunday we were standing by the guns and giving the Devil all he wanted of
red-hot truth in an old worldly camp meeting. Our
co-workers were three local men, two were cigarette
suckers and the other was a good man but on the fence.

They gave me the first Sunday afternoon service. I
suppose they were thinking that it would be a hard
one after folks had crammed their stomachs full of
chicken and gotten sleepy. Well, glory to God. I am
satisfied that was one afternoon service when they
did not sleep. The Lord loaded me so full that I
could not say it fast enough. The next shot I had
was a good one on Tuesday night. The Lord gave
us among the seekers that night a young married
couple. The young fellow prayed clear through and
is now preaching the same rugged truth in one of
our Holiness churches. Also among the seekers was
the wife of the preacher who was on the fence. She

was there for the Blessing, and when she struck fire she jumped to her feet with the glory spread across her countenance and wanted to know where her husband was. While he was coming on the scene from the back of the tabernacle wondering, I suppose, what kind of a spell we had put on his wife, she was clapping her hands and crying and laughing all at once, saying over and over, "He's come! He's come!" When she saw her husband, she threw her arms around his neck and cried and laughed and between shouts said, "He's come!" I'll never forget the glory on that woman's face; and, too, I'll never forget his actions. He grabbed her hands in disgust and put them down, turned on his heel and went to the rear of the tabernacle *to deal with folks about their souls.* It is strange how some preachers get so interested in souls when the fire is falling.

They gave me only one more service after what they termed such a fanatical demonstration. Well, I made up my mind that if it were the last shot I had better use the heavy artillery of heaven; and I did. Those two preachers were so mad they were chewing their old cuds all week and spitting "brown gravy" all over the camp ground. How they did scorch us from the pulpit and would not even let wife and me sing. Well, if we could not sing or preach we could pray, and we did. And before the thing was over the preacher that was on the fence got over the fence and right on the honey side.

While in New York State I had answered a woman's ad that had appeared in a certain paper, for an evan-

gelist. It gave her name and the address as Buffalo
City, Tennessee. Thinking that perhaps I would do,
I wrote, addressing her as the paper stated. After
several weeks I received an answer. First of all she
was puzzled to know how I had found out about them
way down in the mountains of Tennessee. She said
that she had not written any such ad to the paper
but had merely asked the editor to pray that they
might have a revival. The second puzzle was how the
letter ever reached her since there was no such post-
office and never had been; that it was not a city but
a small hamlet of half a dozen houses, and that the
only people that knew it by the name of Buffalo were
the old-timers who had lived there for years, the town
being named thus because someone had' shot a buffalo
at that spot. It was all a mystery to her, but she
stated that they were in need of a revival meeting,
and it seemed strangely providential the way things
had worked out. She went on to state that her husband was not a Christian, but rather given to drink
and the making of moonshine, and though a good-
hearted man, yet she could not depend on him for
financial help. They would be glad to have me come
but could not promise us one cent; all they would do
would be their best.

After corresponding with her several times I felt
impressed to go, and decided to trust the Lord to
provide the way there and the way home again. It
was Saturday; we were to leave Monday and all I
had was a tank full of gas in old "Lizzy". I had figured the distance as about a thousand miles and de-

cided that at the best it would cost us about $15.00 for gas and oil. Before the day was over a certain woman handed me five dollars of her tithe money. I appreciated it immensely, but five was not fifteen, and then I needed more for food and lodging. On top of our financial embarrassment we had invited another party to go with us expecting that he would be better fixed than we were. All day Sunday we looked for someone in the church to slip us something, for we had been praying earnestly and believing that it would come. After the Lord had tried our faith as by fire, the last thing Sunday night we had ten dollars given to us. With fifteen dollars we only had enough for gas and oil. Wife said, "Are you going?" "Well," I said, "we'll start and trust the Lord to see us thru."

Monday morning we were off bright and early on a new venture of faith. We drove hard all day and ate three square meals, never saying a word to D——, the third party. We knew that he did not have but a little change and that he would not have gone if he had known our financial status. Being ignorant of the seriousness of matters along this line, he was buying candy and soda all along the way.

By nine o'clock at night we were in Roanoke, Va., a distance of over four hundred miles since we left home at five in the morning. The next serious question that confronted us was that of lodging. How could we afford to spend money for that when we were so short; yet, if we did not we would have to make some excuse and the truth would leak out. We had decided to tell no one. We knew, too, that if he found out our true state, he would be pessimistic and throw cold water on our faith, and we did not feel as though it was strong enough to stand that. Of course if it had been the kind Elijah had on Mt. Carmel, water would have made it stronger; but it was not.

After some time Wife spoke of a place to lodge. "Well," D—— spoke up, "you don't need to stop on my account for I can sleep in the car." What a loop-hole. Wife said, "Well, I feel that I'll be all right to sleep in the car also; I don't see the need of spending the money." It was all settled. However, we did not do much sleeping but rode nearly all night.

In the morning we stopped at a garage, filled up with gas, and washed the sleep out of our eyes, had some good southern hot cakes for breakfast and were off for the day.

It was nearing the supper hour and, after filling up with gas, I had a little change left. We all very agreeably decided that we were not very hungry, so spent fifteen cents for some crackers and called that our supper. Of course things are not always what they are called.

We were very tired and estimated that we had nearly a hundred miles to go. It was after dark, and we could not see the road very well but took for granted that we were going over a bridge. Rattle, rattle, rattle went the boards. In a few seconds we noticed that at the end of the bridge was a pole across with a light on it. "A toll bridge!" I exclaimed to my wife in an undertone. Our hearts fairly stopped beating. A man stepped out of a little house and asked for twenty-five cents. I was sure I did not have it so called to D—— who was in the back seat half asleep. "Have you got a quarter in change?" "No," he said, "I guess you'll have to break a dollar." I leaned back and punched him to let him know that I was, commonly speaking, "BROKE". That woke him up in a hurry. He went to digging in every pocket, and so did I, and between us we gathered up twenty cents. The old bridge-keeper grunted a little and let us through.

Well, D—— did not sleep any more; he was awake all over and let us know that he would have never come had he known our financial condition.

We had not driven more than twenty-five miles when we were on another bridge, and it was a toll bridge. Then D—— went at it again, "Ridiculous to start out with so little money." Well, we did n't know what to do; we could n't very well turn around on the bridge, so made up our minds that we would go on and see what the Lord would do for us in the emergency. When we arrived at the other end of the bridge, the pole was up; but there was a light in the house. I stopped and tooted, but no one responded. I got out and looked in but could see no one. We had done our part so got in and went on. Of course we could laugh over it when we found no one there and said the Lord must have put a deep sleep on the fellow. We went on giving God the glory. When I returned a few days later, the keeper could n't under-

stand why he had not heard us. I told him I understood it, and paid him the quarter.

We drove on about fifteen miles further, and right
back into the mountains. It was a weird place; we
had heard of the bootleggers and of some of the
shootings that had gone on in such places and were
somewhat afraid to be prowling around at such an
hour. We rode up and down one road several times
trying to see a light in one of the few houses. We
had stopped at a couple houses but could arouse no
one but the dog; so very cautiously we moved on.

We were dead tired; our eyes bloodshot and our
minds numb (having driven about forty hours with
only two or three short naps. We pulled up in front
of a country store about ten-thirty and parked, and
with the moonlit southern sky as a canopy and a
gentle warm breeze to cool our burning dusty brows,
we each found a spot to our own liking and turned
in for the night.

When we awoke in the morning about seven-thirty
with the sun beaming in our faces, wife was curled
up on the back seat, I was on the running board with
its impression well stamped up and down my spine,
while D—— was walking up and down like one on
picket duty, and thinking it all over I guess. We
measured the gas and had one-half gallon, and D——
found one cent in his coat pocket; this constituted
our margin.

We inquired of some passers by and were directed
to the place that we had been hunting so desperately

the night before, it being only about six miles from our night's lodging place, in front of the store.

We met Sister W——, the woman with whom we had corresponded. She was a little woman, unassuming and with a saintly face. Her husband was a rather tall, raw-boned Kentuckian. They had ten children, strong and robust, and with great markings of intelligence, some of whom were Christians.

We were soon informed that a tent had been secured and would be put up, the news of the meeting had been spread around and that, as soon as we were rested, the meeting could be started.

We noticed that Mr. W—— had taken quite an interest in it and we began to pray that God would give us his soul in that meeting. His good wife had been laying the case before God for twenty years.

The meeting began and the people came from all directions. We had never seen anything like it before. They did not come in limousines, or even Fords, but most of them on horse-back or mule-back, and over roads that could not be driven over with a car. Just about dusk we would see them coming from all directions. Here would be a woman on an old long-eared mule with a small baby in her lap and two of three little tots up behind her, hanging on for dear life. Let me say, too, that they do not ride astride, but with side-saddle like women should. Of course many of them are not wonderfully educated, but they have some woman decency. Would it not be fine if some of our more refined people would take a few lessons from them along this line?

Night after night they would come, two and three
hundred strong after a hard day's work. It was not
a side show nor a circus but Gospel meetings. It
did our hearts good to see such an interest in revival
meetings; surely these people appreciate the message
of salvation. We had seekers from the very first
service, and they were seekers, too. They did not
come to that old mourner's bench to look around,
but to mourn, Amen!—and then to laugh and shout
and praise the Lord.

We noticed after a few services that Mr. W—— did
not seem to be so interested and sat near the back of
the tent. A certain night conviction was on heavy,
and there had been several seekers that had prayed
through. Some folks had gone home when Sister
W—— went back to her husband and talked with
him some; and to the surprise of all he got to his
feet and came forward, but sat on the front seat instead of kneeling at the altar. Sister W—— dropped
on her knees beside him and began to pray; other
Christians did likewise, while he sat with his head in
his hands. After a long season of prayer she looked
up and asked him to get on his knees, and he did.
I was surprised at his promptness to obey, knowing
him to be all man, and having a strong mind of his
own; but dear Sister W—— had wrestled the thing
out in prayer that day. Another season of prayer
and still no signs of him getting through. Thank
God that faith, true faith, does not go by signs.
Sister W—— said to him, "Pray, L——." He began
to pray but rather half-heartedly and in undertones.

In a little while he said, "Come on, wife, I'll pray
when we get home." "No, no," she said, "you have
told me that before. Pray!" And he began in the
same way, in undertones. Then he said, "We had better go home, the children will be sleepy." "No," she
said, "pray L——," and repeated it again. Finally
he said, "I'm all through, wife." She said, "L——,
don't you think my Lord will let me know when you
are through?" And she went to praying more earnestly than ever.

One of the women stepped up and said, Sister
W——, you had better stop now; you are getting exhausted." She looked up and said, "My husband is
going to be saved here tonight or you will take me
home a dead woman." And then such agonizing and
soul-travail as I have seldom heard. After quite a
few minutes of such soul anguish we, who were kneeling by, noticed that the color was leaving her cheeks,
her lips turned blue, and the great drops of perspiration stood on her forehead. Well, it surely did look
like she was about ready to expire, but God was in
the place mightily and not one dared to stir. Mr.
W—— looked up, and when he caught sight of his
wife in apparently a dying condition, it struck him
like a dagger. The tears gushed out of his eyes, and
he began to pray like a storm. What repenting! It
was not many minutes until the burden rolled away,
and his soul struck fire. He jumped to his feet and
with face aglow, he shouted, "I'm saved, wife, I'm
saved"! By that time her strength had come back
and she was on her feet shouting with him. In an

instant about seven of the ten children were all trying to hug him at one time. What a hugging match, tears running, shouts ascending, while the old mountains were echoing and re-echoing the sound to the heavens!

When he finally emerged from the happy family, he gave his testimony and that brought another round of Hallelujahs from all who were present.

When he was able to get away from the happy throng, he stepped outside the tent and poured out a half-pint of whiskey and threw the bottle in the weeds; went into his pockets and got out every piece of tobacco and threw them away, and has never touched it again.

The next morning he went to the barn and put an axe in several kegs of moonshine. Praise God, it was worth riding four hundred hours to see such a transformation.

I do not know how many got through in the meeting, but I do know that the country was ablaze with the revival fire. One of the sons, who was not a Christian, prayed through; two of the girls were sanctified; and at the present time one of the boys is preparing for the ministry and one of the girls is ready for the field of evangelism.

CHAPTER XI

PASTOR OF A HOLINESS CHURCH

Upon our return home after a series of meetings, we found that a certain mission in our home city had been turned into an independent Holiness church. The building had been renovated and remodeled and made quite a respectable place in which to worship. We were delighted to see such a change in the place and happy to know that the city was having a Holiness church to minister to its welfare. We found a preacher in charge, but only temporarily, as he had his own church to look after several miles away.

We had intended to remain in the evangelistic work, seeing that God was putting His seal upon our humble efforts. One evening after the meeting Bro. C—— said that he could not come up any more and would like to have us take care of the work until Bro. E—— returned. (Bro. E—— had been responsible for the renovating and starting of the new work.)

It was all new to us, but we consented. I cannot say that we felt especially led of the Lord to supply, but as we had no meetings at that time, it seemed providentially arranged. Well, we had a nice clean place in which to preach and plenty in our souls to preach about, but there was no congregation, that is, we had no membership, no one to feel any responsibility, and just a few folks that came in when they had no place particularly to go.

We made up our mind that we would do our best, and prove God. We commenced giving the truth in our awkward way and the Lord began sending in hungry souls. The first few weeks there were several happy finders at the altar and the congregation was increasing, a number of them were coming regularly. This was a great encouragement to us. We had taken the work with much fear and trembling, realizing our inability. After we had thundered away for about two months, Bro. E—— returned and gave us a few days' meeting, and, by consent of the congregation which the Lord had sent us, we were appointed to take the work permanently.

Surely God set his seal on it and poured out His Spirit in a marveluos way. We had the blessed opportunity of ministering to our own loved ones who had so recently got into the Fountain. It was just wonderful to see them grow spiritually and get under the load and help us lift. The new converts were on fire and would pull the glory down until the place was filled with the power of God. Many times there would be four or five slain by the power while seekers wept their way through to victory.

It was not long, with such singular manifestations of God's presence, until the seats began to fill up, some coming out of curiosity and others with hungry hearts. With the fire burning and the glory on some, who we thought were our friends, began to cry, "Wild Fire! Fanaticism!" Well, if it was, I say, "Lord, give us more of it."

I have found in my short experience that with the presence of God in the camp, the finances will take care of themselves also. When folks are blessed, it is no task for them to tithe. They count it a privilege, and then give their love offerings besides. The money came in without effort and many times we had a good balance in the treasury.

On a certain occasion we planned a revival meeting, to be held by the above mentioned Bro. E———. The saints were in good shape and we were ready to put our shoulder to the wheel and push the thing for God and Holiness. If I remember, correctly, the meeting broke through to victory in the early part and swept on with great power. Sinners were converted, believers were sanctified, and the saints were shouting happy. The neighborhood around became so stirred that they crowded the doors to look in, while some of them ventured to take seats in the rear. It seemed as though the very atmosphere were impregnated with the Presence of Divinity. Praise God for such experiences! Surely we could say, "The slain of the Lord were many."

During this series of meetings, I received a call to preach in a certain church about thirty miles from the city. It was the last service of the revival and I wanted to be at my own church, but had promised that I would be in P——— for Sunday morning service.

We stayed at our own church for the Saturday night meeting and left a little early on Sunday for our appointment. When we were leaving, the evangelist made the remark that if "Lizzy" spoke on the way, like Balaam's ass, we should turn and come back.

It was a dismal, dreary morning; quite a heavy fog hung low and made it very bad driving. We had not gone very far, perhaps ten miles, when the car began to boil and steam. We put in all the water it would hold and went on. In a few minutes time the fog had turned to a fine rain and began freezing on the wind shield. I think I must have got out a half dozen times and scraped it off, but still we went on. I began to feel that we were out of order but, wanting to fulfill my promise, I drove on. In a little while the old Ford began missing; first it was on three cylinders and then on two. Then it began boiling and before I could get to a place to put in some water something exploded and enveloped us in a cloud of smoke. Before I could get stopped, Wife had the door open and was on her way out. After the smoke cleared away and we could get our bearings, we found that the hose from the radiator to the engine had bursted under the pressure of the steam. Well, "Lizzy" had surely spoken as plainly as Balaam's ass. We bowed our heads and asked the Lord to forgive us for being so persistent and running ahead of the Spirit. We got the water hose fixed, turned "Lizzy's" nose toward home and she ran beautifully all the way and without a skip in the motor. We were hardly started in the home direction until it stopped raining and we did not have to get out once to clean the ice from the windshield.

I learned a great lesson in this experience and made up my mind to obey the leadings of the Lord. regardless of what people might think or say.

When we arrived home the evangelist asked us if "Lizzy" spoke, and we humbly confessed the truth. Amen! I went to the telephone and called the preacher that I was to help in meetings. What a voice on the other end of the wire! It sounded like a bear rather than a man. I knew immediately that he was mad. It was quite evident that he did not have the Blessing. I explained the situation, but he only grumbled and let me know what an embarrassing position I had put him in, for he had not prepared any sermon for the service.

Though the Lord had made it plain to us that we were to return to our own church and be there for the afternoon and evening service yet I did not see why. The afternoon service was very good but nothing spectacular. We came up to the evening meeting and still nothing unusual. While the brother was preaching, perhaps half-way through, a burden fell on my soul like a load of lead. It was for a young person who had gone away to prepare for the ministry and was not within a thousand miles of the church.

The burden came so unexpectedly and with such weight that it crushed us under its pressure. What agony of soul! With a thud it knocked us to the floor and took away our physical strength. For over an hour we groaned and travailed, unable to know anything of what was taking place around us. All we could see was the young man apparently on the brink of perdition. After a long while the burden was lifted and there came that sweet assurance that God had heard and answered prayer. Our strength returned and we were able to get to our feet, to find that many had prayed through and God had poured out of His spirit on the congregation.

With such an experience, I was satisfied why the Lord wanted me back in my own church for that service. We had labored with the young man and led him to the Lord and God seemed to want to use us to travail in pain again for him.

About the last of the next week I received a short note from him saying that he was sick in the hospital and had had a very serious time of it the Sunday before. How I rejoiced that God had helped me to be obedient to His leading! A few months later when he returned from school he told me that he had lost out in his experience at the time of the incident above and was under financial pressure and discouragement. Not wanting any one to know his true condition he had determined to end it all and had taken eight or ten aspirin tablets. He said that the very Sunday that I had been so burdened they did not expect him to live and had him under close observation and treatment all day. Praise God for the realities of the Gospel! We truly are members one of another, and when one suffers we all suffer.

I do believe that if there were more faithful Christians upon whom God could place the burden of prayer there would not be so many that would backslide under pressure and temptation. Let us be faithful in the ministry of prayer, realizing that we are our brother's keeper.

One night during an altar service, the blessing of God fell upon many and the Shekinah glory was impregnating the atmosphere. Among the Christians at the altar was a colored boy and also a man who had been raised in the State of Maryland. I never heard the latter express himself as being especially prejudiced toward the colored race but naturally there would remain some of the impressions of early days. It was not long until the tide rose to such a height that every one that was blessable was swept in, including the colored boy, too. I finally looked up and to my surprise the colored boy and the Marylander had arms around each others necks and the tears were streaming—black tears and white ones were all running together. Well, glory to God! The blessing of His presence breaks down the middle wall of partition and makes us members of the same family. Amen!

A certain young man had come about two hundred miles to attend the church. He sold all he had but an old Ford, packed his wife and baby in, and arrived ready to settle down where the Blessing was falling. He had never seen anything of the power of God, and the first Sunday morning while the glory was on and folks prostrated, Bro. R—— just about decided that he should have stayed where he came from. His first impression was "Fanaticism", but in spite of the feelings and arguments that he was presenting to several of the young men, he stayed around. I don't think it was more than a few weeks until he began to see his need of being sanctified and bowed at the altar. After seeking for a while he suddenly jumped to his

feet exclaiming, "He's come! He's come!" And what
a glorious shine was on his countenance. After pa-
rading up and down the aisle several times with his
long slender form, and clapping his large bony hands,
he fell at the altar again and almost instantly he was
overcome with the power of God, or what he had
thought was fanaticism a few weeks before. When
he finally gained his strength he arose to his feet and
staggered and reeled like a drunken man. The Lord
certainly did give him an abundant measure. I saw
immediately that he would need help in order to get
home, even though it was only a few houses from
the church where he had rented rooms. I managed
to get him to the house and while he stood on the
step reeling and laughing with the joy of the Lord
and going in every pocket endeavoring to find his key,
I noticed that he was leaning against the door bell.
Before we could get the door open the landlady came
and got a good look at Bro. R—— filled with the glory
of the Lord, intoxicated with new wine. She certainly
did look, too, both at him and then at me, for I had
taken him there and introduced him as a fine Christian man, and now here I was taking him home apparently drunk. We were so happy that "none of these
things moved us." Bro. R—— has never opposed
demonstrations from that day to this.

While we were pastoring this church, Wife became
anemic and finally was so bad that the doctor said it
was imperative that she have a blood transfusion. It
happened, or rather God had it planned I believe,
that L——, the daughter of Bro. W——, who had

been converted in the tent meeting in Tennessee the year before, had come to visit us. When we began to talk of a transfusion she spoke up and said that she would gladly give some of hers if it would do.

The day arrived and all three of us went to the hospital and when they tested L's— blood it was identically the same. They placed her on one table and Wife on the other, in the operating room, and proceeded. As they began pushing a large needle into the veins of L's—— arm, the doctor said, "That hurts, Miss W——, doesn't it?" With the muscles of her face tense with the pain, she replied, "I can stand it for Sister Bradley." The doctor was amazed at such love. "Greater love hath no man than this, that a man lay down his life for his friend," was the only thing I could think of as they told me about it. With this comes the thought of what Jesus paid for our redemption. Wife said as the blood was drawn from L's—— arm and the color left her cheeks and lips, she could see it as it flowed into a large funnel-shaped bottle, sparkling with life as it flowed.

Let me say here to the sinner that may read these lines, the precious blood of Jesus flowed from His riven side nearly two thousand years ago, and as it sparkled with Divine life for every one then, it is still efficacious for the "Whosoever will." It has never coagulated nor lost any of its power. Praise His name! Will you not plunge in and be made every whit whole?

After they had finished drawing it from L's—— arm, they turned to wife and began to insert the needle into her arm, but with very little success. They tried five or six times but the veins being so empty had collapsed and it was impossible to get the needle located properly. Finally in desperation, and after several of the doctors had talked together, they decided that they would try once more. It meant to administer the life-giving blood or it would only be a matter of a short while when her life would be extinct.

Let me say again, that many a sinner is being confronted with the same serious condition, spiritually speaking. It means certain, eternal death if you do not have the precious Blood applied to your poor sinful heart. It is all ready and God will now by His Spirit administer it to you.

They tried it once more and, praise God, they were able to get the needle in the vein. Wife said that as soon as the blood was released from the bottle she could feel the warm stream going into her arm and being carried directly to the heart, and when it struck the little organ it began to pick up like a machine when you feed the gas. Notice, she said she felt it. Every one that has the precious blood of Christ applied will feel it, and know the work is done. Thank God for a real know-so salvation. The blood had not been in her system but a few minutes when the reaction began; she broke out with a rash and began shaking like a leaf. She shook so hard that the bed fairly moved on the floor. The nurse got on one side and I on the other and laid across her body to keep her from shaking, but she continued to shake and the nurse and myself shook with her. My Brother, every soul that gets old-time Bible salvation will not only know it, but there will be a reaction. There will be a rash of glory on their countenance and a spell of expression, whether by laughing, shouting, crying or some other way, and no one will be able to stop it. In fact, it will have a similar effect on those who are sympathetic with the experience.

It was but a few weeks when Wife's condition became alarming again. She was bedfast and it was necessary for us to call in a nurse and a second doctor for consultation. The final decision was an operation. I was willing, but penniless, having spent all I had for the nurse and the blood transfusion. Feeling that God would see us through, I consented and so did my wife.

In the evening before she was to go, I sat in her room and we talked over the past. It seemed as though we were talking for the last time. After discussing material problems, she approached the spiritual. I asked her concerning her experience and she said there was just one thing that bothered her. She had never given up the wearing of her wedding ring. It had been her mother's, who had died when she was a child, and she had always justified herself in wearing it. She had taken it off once or twice but only for a short time; the longing for it would become so intense that she had put it on again. It was somewhat different now; she was taking inventory for eternity and God was faithfully showing her that it was impeding her spiritual progress and standing in her way. She took it off, and when she did the blessing began to fall like dew upon our souls. We prayed and sang

and talked, looked into each others faces and knew
that if it were our last such season together we would
meet on the shores of Fair Deliverance. Before morning she had several attacks, and once we thought she
had crossed the line of worlds, but God was good and
has spared her until this present time.

The operation was over and she was getting along
well. The question that confronted me now was where
would I get the money to meet the bill. The Lord
had always provided and though the waves of doubt
were trying to swamp my frail craft, I kept my eyes on
"the Author and Finisher of my faith."

I was planning on going to see my wife, as I did
every day, but I found that my financial status was
very low and that I lacked ten cents of having enough
to get across the bridge to Philadelphia and back.
The toll was twenty-five cents each way for a car and
I only had forty cents. It seemed as though it was
taking about as much faith for me to trust for that
ten cents as it was for the amount of the hospital
bill. I had planned on going to class meeting first
and then to Philadelphia. A friend of mine who lived
in Philadelphia decided to go to the class with me
and then we would ride over the bridge together.
With such plans I felt that he would pay the bridge
toll one way and I would be all right. During the
course of the meeting the blessing began to fall and I
presume it got too hot for G——, for when I looked
for him he had gone, and so had my hopes of the
bridge toll. I have found that just as sure as we get
a leaning post instead of trusting God, He is sure to

remove it, thereby keeping us with our faith centered in Himself. I turned my eyes heavenward and started with my faith built this time on the Rock of Ages. When I got in the car I saw two elderly women standing on the church steps, whose home was in Philadelphia. They were poor in this world's goods but rich in grace. They climbed in and away we went. I paid the toll of twenty-five cents and held tight to the fifteen that I had left. When we arrived at the destination, the women alighted from the car and while they were making ready to go one of them reached out her hand and said, "The Lord told me to give you this" and handed me a ten-cent piece—just what I needed. Well, Glory to God! He said He would supply every need and He did just to the very penny.

I presume most folks would be too proud to hand some one ten cents; no doubt would say, "Well, if I could not give more than that I would not give at all." Let me say, reader, if God lays it on your heart to give, no matter how small it may be, do it, and God will be glorified and your soul will be blessed and the other party's need will be met. It pays to obey the Spirit.

The day before Wife was to leave the hospital, we were still trusting with not a penny in sight for the bill which had to be paid before I could take her home. A godly old man was visiting her. We sat and talked, praised God, and got blessed together. Before he went he rather cautiously asked us how we expected to meet our bill. Well, we told him we were trusting God and that he would send the right man along. We were confident that he did not possess any of this world's goods, so did not hesitate to speak our mind. He raised his hand to Heaven and, with shining face and tears streaming, said, "I'm the man." Well, we had a shouting time; the nurse came in, looked around and went out again. Praise God, when we needed ten cents the Lord sent it, when we needed a hundred dollars He sent it. And He has been supplying every need since.

CHAPTER XII

EVANGELISTIC EXPERIENCES

After having definite direction from the Lord to return to the evangelistic field, we resigned our pastorate in Camden and prepared to go to our first meeting in New York state, which was about two hundred and fifty miles from home.

The day before we were to leave, the Ford showed some symptoms of a bad spell of sickness; there was a peculiar hum in the rear and it sounded as though all it needed was a new one. I drove into a garage and invited one of the mechanics to diagnose the case and give me the cost of repairs. He did it, and told me that the rear was worn out, needed a new one and would cost me fifteen dollars to have it repaired. I do not know how he knew, but fifteen dollars was all that I had to start the trip the next day. He added to all of the above information that it would not be safe to drive it at all.

Wife and I talked it over together and decided that we would put the old car in the Lord's hands and trust Him to provide for its repair or perform a miracle on it. Praise Him, He did the latter.

The next day, my wife, a singer and I started on our trip. For the first thirty miles it sounded as if a swarm of bees were following us, but on we went trusting in the promise that has never failed.

Shortly we noticed that the noise had ceased and I must testify for "old Lizzy" that I never heard that sound again. We traveled about ten thousand miles with it after that and never spent a penny to have the rear repaired. I am persuaded that God is interested in the little everyday affairs of His children.

We were holding meetings for the Volunteers of America in a certain city. We had thundered out the truth for nearly two weeks, and there had not been a single soul at the altar nor any signs of a break. We had prayed, fasted and labored hard but seemingly we were praying to a god of stone. How the devil did attack us with his demon forces while we held onto the Word of God.

It was Sunday and the last day of the meeting. They had no morning service but had advertised meetings for afternoon and evening. While we were waiting before God that morning with our feeble faith trying to penetrate the awful clouds of doubt that were trying to hide His blessed face, we looked up and told Him that if He never blessed us again we would preach and sing because of what He had already done for us. We had hardly gotten the words out of our mouth when the heavens opened and "God came down our souls to greet, while glory crowned the mercy seat."

We hurried off to service. When we went into the hall the crowd was so large that we could hardly get thru to the platform. We not only had a crowded house but the "smoke of God's presence filled the place". When the altar call was given the penitents lined the rail and what a time of victory God gave us! There was but a short intermission between the afternoon and evening services, and then there was another great victory.

We have learned that our "extremity is God's opportunity", and that He never fails to fulfill His promise.

A few months later we were called to a certain church in the same city. It was a Holiness church and most every member professed the Blessing, but few of them possessed it. The first few days everything went fine as is quite usual, then we struck a snag. We were able to recognize, by the help of the Spirit, that there was friction between the people and the pastor; this because of a lack of oil. One cannot even expect to run church machinery without keeping it well lubricated. The presence of the blessed Holy Ghost, of which oil is a type, is necessary to keep things in harmony. Nothing is quite so hard on the nervous system as discord; nothing is quite so soothing as harmony. As it is in the natural so it is in the spiritual; hence God has given the oil of gladness to keep our souls lubricated, and the church in a place where she can broadcast notes of harmony to a world that is dying for love.

After preaching plain, unvarnished truths to the church for about a week, we decided that we would have to employ some other method; after waiting on the Lord to know just what to do next we were led very definitely.

It was Wednesday night and quite a few of the members had gathered in the prayer room before service. We all knelt to pray, but there we stayed for quite a while without any one opening his mouth. The place was like a funeral house; the atmosphere was heavy and so were the hearts of the people. Finally I decided to break the spell. I started to pray, said about a dozen words and could go no further. Another started but stopped just as abruptly. After we had stayed in that frigid zone for about thirty minutes and I felt my soul getting greatly chilled, I decided to go to a little warmer climate. One by one they filed out into the main auditorium and sat down like deaf mutes.

We did not feel disposed to preach long to that crowd but announced that we wanted to see all of the members at the close of the service. After the visitors had gone we told them in few words that if they did not straighten out among themselves we would pack our bags and leave immediately. Then we ordered an old-fashioned closed class meeting, starting with Brother A——, the pastor. He took a very humble position apologizing to the church for some things and going to a few personally. One by one they arose and acknowledged their faults, took the blame that belonged to them and in about ten minutes tears were flowing and faces were glowing. The men were hugging one another while the women were fixing up little difficulties that had arisen between them; people and preacher were feeling fine.

From then on the meeting just ran itself or rather the Holy Ghost took charge of the program. Especially on the last Sunday did God pour out His Spirit in an unusual way. It was the afternoon service; the congergation was fair, but the atmosphere seemed impregnated with the presence of Divinity. While wife and I sang with the anointing upon us heavily, many wept. Without reading a lesson I began to exhort, my soul being exceedingly heavy for the lost. For about ten minutes the Lord poured the hot truth upon them and without any formal altar call they started coming, broken and contrite. Praise God, no one had to drag them there nor coax them to pray, but in agony of soul they prayed their hearts out and one by one struck the Rock of Ages. Some were crying, some were laughing, some were shouting, some were walking the aisles, while others remained in their seats as if stunned by a charge of electricity. Glory to God, He will honor His Word!

While the waves of glory swept over the congregation a dear saint whose two daughters had prayed thru, stood at the altar with tears falling like rain and her face shining. The power of God struck her to the floor with a thud. Like the morning dew settles softly on the green vegetation, a hallowed peace came upon all; the shouting ceased instantly, and we sat in the presence of the Lord of hosts in holy awe.

I have come to the conclusion that no revival is better than a spurious one; I would sooner suffer total defeat than to have a victory that is superficial and fleshly, one that has to be worked up by mere emotionalism. When the saints are in harmony, God will pour out the blessing upon them.

In the spring of 1928 we were planning to go South for meetings. We only had one in Tenessee but felt that God was dealing and knew that others would be forthcoming. My dear grandmother, who has since gone to her reward, was in need of a change; so we decided to have her go along.

We started early one morning; it was Grandma's first long trip and she was bright and happy. We sang and talked together and had a splendid time the first two days. The third day it was raining and our old Model T Ford was not in very good shape for a rain storm. It was a touring car and had a top on it which was much like a sieve. We had not gone many miles when the top began to leak and wife would have to mop the ceiling every few minutes to keep the water from dripping on us. Finally it rained so hard and so long that we decided to make some changes; so we put up the umbrella and tilted back so that the water ran down into the back seat. This kept us quite comfortable, since we all sat in the front. Poor Grandma had never had such experiences before and every little while she would say, "Floyd, do you think old 'Lizzy' will hold up until we get there." While it rained and the roof leaked we sang and praised the Lord. Then Grandma would say, "I don't believe you children have sense enough to worry."

We arrived safely and were received cordially. The Lord gave us a precious time with the saints but little was accomplished among the sinners. Things were tight financially and as a result the offering was small, in fact, not enough to get us back to New Jersey. We had no other meetings in view. When we were ready to go, and were bidding good-bye to the folks with whom we had been staying, we noticed one of their girls, a kindly, spirit-filled character of about eighteen, go into the house hurriedly,. When she returned she slipped a bag to wife and said, "I would like to give you more, Sister Bradley, but this is all I have. I hope it will help some." When we looked at it later we found that it was twenty-five pennies. She did what she could; that is all God requires of any of us. I would sooner have a few gifts from praying people than the wealth of the wicked. We do not know how long she had been saving that amount nor what she had intended to buy with it, but like the woman with the alabaster box of ointment, she gave willingly what she had. Let us be faithful stewards whether over much or little.

We stopped in Knoxville over night and learned that there was a mission about thirty miles east of there, among the poor whites that would be glad to have us preach for them over the week end. We were not long finding the place and the people who had charge of it. We were entertained by different families for dinner and supper and, after the service in the evening, we were escorted to our lodging place.

We stayed with a dear sister who had a shining face
and clear testimony, but my what living conditions!
As it was dark we did not spend much time inspect-
ing but crawled into bed. We had what they would
call, I presume, a semi-private room. I mean by that
that it was not partly private but private part of the
time. There was no lock on the door and the serious
part of the whole situation was that you did not
know just when you were going to have privacy. As
we observed in the morning our room seemed to be
the main thoroughfare to the second floor.

The room had two beds, one of which was given to
wife and me, while the other one was for Grandma.
We were well able to arrange that but when it came
to having some one's else Grandma in the room
with us, it made it somewhat embarrassing. On Sunday the woman's mother came to visit. When it was
time to retire Grandma was informed that Grandma
Number Two was to sleep with her. She said, "I
don't know whether Floyd will like that or not."
"Well, we can't help it if he does not. That's the way
we do here," she replied. So all decided that since
we were in Rome we might as well do as Rome did.

I am inclined to think that Grandma was speaking
two for herself and one for me; she was quite partial
toward cleanliness and apparently Grandma Number
Two was just the opposite. Instead of them giving
us regular bed covering we had old dirty feather
mattresses for covering. But I must say one thing:
I did not feel a single one of those pesty little fel-

lows that we had met in some homes although they looked a great deal cleaner than theirs.

There was quite a family of children. The smaller ones up to about four years old were not very well trained and that in many ways, some of which I would not dare to write. One way was in eating. They ate with their hands and, as they tried to cram it into their mouths, they put more on their shirt fronts than in their stomachs. All of this was not much of a stimulant to appetite. But in spite of the dirt they were a healthy group of children.

One woman in the community told us that she always gave her children soup as soon as they were born, even before they had milk. Wife asked how she made the soup. Her reply was, "Side pork, potatoes, onions and roasting ears." No wonder they are such sturdy little chaps. I'm inclined to believe that it is the survival of the fittest.

We observed another thing that may be of interest and perhaps if adopted will be a great time-saver for the average housewife: Their method of washing dishes is somewhat different from ours. They had a large wash-tub on the back porch which was full of water and probably had not been changed for several days. The dishes were gathered from the table, carried to the back porch and dumped into the huge dishpan where they were allowed to soak for a while. Of course all of the scraps and leavings on the plates would float to the top. These were scooped off and thrown out to the chickens. When they had soaked a while they were pulled out and wiped off with a dish-cloth that looked more like a scrub rag, and were ready for the next meal.

In spite of Grandma's desire for cleanliness she sang and praised the Lord the whole time we stayed there. She said, "Children, I never have realized what I have to be thankful for."

On Monday morning after having prayer with the family we bade them good-bye and left. How they did cry! They told us how much our visit had meant to them, and said they wanted to meet us in heaven. We have never seen them since but trust that we shall meet them where the environment will be satisfactory to all.

The Spirit directed us to Ashville, N. C., where we got in touch with a preacher at Hendersonville who wanted a meeting. We were soon located and ready to pitch battle against the forces of the enemy. We were entertained by a godly woman, whose husband and sister were very much opposed to Holiness teaching, and so they were very antagonistic toward us. The sister was really hateful and did not hesitate to show it.

I'm so glad that the plan of the Gospel is not retaliation but perfect love. Surely the Lord did give us wisdom in dealing with that case. As we were enjoying the fullness of the blessing we were able to heap coals of fire on her head. She had utterly refused to attend any of the meetings and, in fact, would hardly converse with us in the home.

During the last two or three days of the meeting we noticed a decided change in her. She said, on

Saturday, that she would go to church with us in the evening if we would take her. Well, Amen! We were more than glad to take her and wondered what was going to take place next. The service was of a deep nature and when the invitation was given who should come to the altar but that very woman, and she prayed thru as beautifully as could be.

We left on Monday and took her about a hundred miles in the northern part of the state to her home. When we left her out her eyes were filled with tears. She felt so badly for the way she had treated us and wished that we could visit her a while. There is nothing that will give us such openings into the hearts of people as Perfect Love.

We were called to a little mining village in West Virginia to hold a meeting. There was no church and the only available place was a schoolhouse. We commenced on Sunday evening with perhaps a dozen people among whom was the school teacher.

We were entertained in the best home in the village. The man was a Catholic and his wife not much of anything. Although it was the best home in town, yet they were poor people and shared with us what they had. The meeting had not been in progress more than five or six nights when Mr. J——, with whom we had been staying, came forward and humbly confessed his need. Then came his wife and two daughters, followed by others. The Lord of hosts surely met us in that little schoolhouse. I do not remember the number of seekers but I do remember the shining faces, among the number a dozen or more fine young people.

We were being entertained at a certain place by a poor family. They were doing their best to give us enough to eat but most of it was potatoes and dried lima beans. We had potatoes and beans, then beans and potatoes for two weeks until we felt pretty well starched. On Saturday we understood that they were going to give us a real treat the next day. Sure enough we heard one of the girls in the yard cutting off the chickens' heads. After they were dressed and ready for cooking, Wife heard the mother say to the daughter, "I haven't anything big enough to cook these in. Get me that kettle on the porch." We had noticed that the mother had been scrubbing the floors in the morning with a kettle for a scrub pail, so wife decided that she had better investigate. Upon looking out of the window she saw the girl take the mop out of the pail, empty the water, swab the bucket out with the dish cloth and dump in the chicken. Wife said, "There goes our chicken dinner." I told her she should not be seeing so much and that I intended to eat some of it anyway.

When the chicken was passed at dinner the next day, I very bravely took a piece. The longer I looked at it the more my stomach rebelled. I ate everything else on my plate but I could not get the courage to eat the chicken. I imagine it was well seasoned with coal dirt, as the one kettle of water had been used to mop three very dirty floors.

CHAPTER XIII

HUMOROUS EXPERIENCES

The life of a traveling preacher or evangelist not only brings him in touch with hard places, sad scenes and touching incidents, but here and there are some things that nearly make one's sides ache with laughter. I will endeavor to relate some such happenings here.

One time while preaching in a rural section we were invited out for dinner with a certain family by the name of F——. My dear grandmother was staying with us at the time so, of course, she was invited too. Mr. F—— set the time and said he would come after us, since they lived on the mountain (literally) and it was impossible to get up with a car.

The day arrived and we were all ready and looking forward to a good time, also a good meal. Every one told us that Mrs. F—— was a wonderful cook and had graduated from a certain Domestic Science School. Mr. and Mrs. F—— were rated as well fixed, financially, and owned the biggest part of the mountain. About 11:30 Mr. F—— arrived to take us to the top of the mountain. When we went out to get in we found a very old open wagon, with two boards across for seats. We managed to climb in and were off.

The only thing I can think of in connection with that wild ride is the story of "The One Horse Shay."

Did I say wild ride? Well, it was all of that. It was not long before we were climbing the mountain, into deep ruts and out again, across streams, thru the woods, over rocks, and all of us hanging on for dear life. Occasionally the mud and partially melted snow, that was still falling, would be thrown into our laps or spattered into our faces. What time was not consumed in holding on, or wiping mud from our faces, we watched the wheels very carefully to see that none rolled off and got lost. It seemed like every wheel was going in a different direction, they were so warped and loose on the axle. Surely it seemed as though the old wagon was about ready to collapse . The harness, which had undoubtedly been all leather at one time, had been repaired and patched until it was about one quarter rope and another quarter fence wire. What was left of the original harness looked as if is was about ready to go on the retired list. Every time the horses would pull us up a grade we wondered which piece would give way first and how fast that old wagon could travel backward. After about thirty or forty minutes of such nerve strain we pulled up into the yard of what they called home. Who should come out to meet us but Mrs. F—— all dressed to receive her company. She came to the wagon and welcomed us in a very gushing manner. What a picture she was! Her dress looked as though she had used it for a scrub cloth, it was to her knees from the bottom up and struck nearly the same average from the top down. Her stockings, what there was of them, went round and round her limbs like a stripe on a barber's pole, with large holes in each heel, or I should say, where the heel had been. Her hair, what was not straggling down her face, was screwed up in a knot and stuck on the extreme end of her head, while a very sharp nose made quite a contrast on the other extreme end.

We observed a lot from the gate to the front door, and I guess it was a good thing, for there was so much to be seen when we got inside that we did not have time to spend scrutinizing Mrs. F——. We were ushered thru one of the filthiest kitchens that I had ever seen and into what was termed the living room, which was not quite so bad. She gave us chairs where we were in full view of the kitchen and pantry. There were two or three children in the room when we entered, one not more than eighteen months, and none of them had more than one garment on and no shoes or stockings. I do not think they ever got thirsty either, for there was a continual stream from the nose to the mouth. What an appetizing sight to look at while dinner was being prepared. In a few minutes in came another, shoeless also, and he had his pet lamb with him. Mr. Lamb made himself right at home, just as though he had been there before, and when his hunger needed appeasing he went to the wall, gnawed the paper loose at the baseboard, tore a strip as high up as he could reach and then chewed it off.

Finally, after trying to make us feel at home, Mrs. F—— began to stir up some biscuits for the meal. While she rolled the dough, one of the little fellows, with an excess nasal discharge, stood at the board and watched her with his nose resting directly on the edge of it. When she finished and those *delicious* hot biscuits were in the oven, she mixed up some icing for a cake that she had baked. While she stood with her back to the bowl, the same little fellow, with the same dirty hands and face, stood behind her scooping out great fingerfuls of icing and shoving them into his mouth.

After all that we had been forced to observe, I don't need to say that we had poor appetites. However, we managed to eat something, though it was little.

When it was time for the baby to take his nap, we saw Mrs. F—— looking under chairs, behind the stove, etc., for his bottle. Finally, she found it, with some milk clinging to the inside, off came the nipple and in a jiffy it was filled up and ready for use, without washing. She grabbed up the little fellow, took him into an adjoining room and dumped him into bed. The lamb followed suit and I presume they were both off for a good nap.

It is needless to say that we did not stay for supper as was pre-arranged, nor did we get our necks broken on the way home, as we feared. We all breathed a sigh of relief when we climbed out of our *limousine* and stepped into the parsonage.

Another experience that makes us thankful we were reared to recognize cleanliness took place while we were being entertained in a certain home in the South.

When we went into the house the odor was not any too inviting and the room to which we were assigned did not look any too clean; but that was where we had been sent, so there was nothing else to do but go and stay. The first meal was in the evening and as it was dark and they used oil lamps, we did not notice many things that the daylight revealed.

After coming home from meeting, it being a hot sultry night, Wife and I both were tired and decided to go right to bed and get a night's rest. Well, we did the former but not the latter. We had not been in bed long when we recognized that the mattress was made of corn stalks and had a hollow place right in the middle. No matter how hard we tried to stay out of that hole, we could not, and the trouble was both got in it at the same time. The room was small, the two windows were small and so was the fresh air. When we were about tired out trying to hang to the edges of the bed and keep out of the hole, and perhaps would have gone to sleep from exhaustion and in spite of the hot weather, we became aware that there were others in the bed besides ourselves. Wife realized it first, when a whole battalion of those little flat-backed pests laid siege to her territory. Raising up on her elbow she said, "There are bugs in this bed." I told her I did not think so, but thought it was her nerves. In a short while they began to attack me, and then I was convinced. We climbed out and lit the lamp and most of them by that time had moved their machine guns under cover and we only found one or two doing picket duty. We executed them. Wife was so tired and weary that she sat down and cried. I tried to comfort her with the fact that it could be worse and told her we had a lot to be thankful for.

We finally crawled in again about four, and were just about asleep when an old hound dog under the window began barking in that weird tone. He would stop and then one about a half mile away would answer. They must have kept that up for an hour, occasionally they would sing a duet. However we managed to get at least a nap before it was time to arise.

We ate breakfast, or rather they served it, and in the daylight we saw more than was good for us, and which did much to take the edge off our appetites.

When we returned at noon we found to our surprise and much to our discomfort that they washed dishes only once a day, and that was after supper. There was one good thing about it, each fellow sat in the same place so that we at least did not have to eat from some one's else plate.

That evening we were invited to another home and took advantage of it.

Most every one knows that the south is a great place for snuff and tobacco. We had not been there long when we found this to be true. In a certain rural school, the school master and about half the class could be seen chewing their cud like an old cow and occasionally, when the saliva would get too plentiful, they would send it to the floor.

There was one woman whom we engaged to do our wash while we stayed in this place. For a week or more I was under the impression that the poor woman had a tumor on her jaw and she surely had my sympathy. I later learned to my surprise that it was not on her jaw but in her jaw and was of a removable nature, in the form of a cud of tobacco. God wonderfully delivered her from that habit the last time we were there.

At the close of a series of meetings in the mountain section of Tennessee, we were invited to spend the evening at a certain home. It was cool weather and the fireplace was burning. We all pulled our chairs around in a semi-circle and near enough to get the warmth without getting burned. It was not long until the men, about three, began whittling off a chew from a big overgrown plug of tobacco and in a short time they were pretty well under motion. Then the women, one by one, began bringing out the little boxes of powdered chocolate, throwing a little under their lip and it was not long until they were in action. Then came the target pratices. First, a man would spit a long brown stream into the fire and we would hear it sizzle and fry, then one of the women would try to beat the preceding record. So it went, first one and then another and all of them leaving their trade mark from where they sat to the fireplace, including their chins.

We stayed until we saw them take several shots apiece and then decided there was no fellowship for us in that circle, though all of them were professing Christians.

CHAPTER XIV

SETTLING VITAL QUESTIONS

There are many questions that confront us daily that demand an immediate answer, while others may be postponed until a more convenient season. Of all questions, the one most vital is that which concerns the immortal soul. This question should have our undivided attention.

God calls once; He may call a number of times, but there comes the last call. The Holy Spirit flashes the danger signal across the pathway, strives with the soul and, after being turned away unheeded, He leaves to return no more.

> "There is a time we know not when,
> A place we know not where,
> That marks the destiny of man,
> For glory or despair.—
>
> "There is a line to us unseen
> That crosses every path,
> The hidden boundary between
> God's mercy and His wrath."

The sinner cannot say "No" to God without his heart growing more calloused. The Christian cannot turn a deaf ear to the call of God, either to a deeper experience or to definite Christian service, without suffering serious loss. God demands our obedience.

In this chapter I feel impressed to record some instances that have come under our own observation during our ministry.

It was in a coal mining section. The meetings had been in progress about a week; the interest was keen and a woman's meeting had been planned for Sunday afternoon with Sister Bradley in charge. During the altar call there were a number of seekers and among them a school teacher. We had met her before, in fact, she had attended the services regularly. She was in possession of a winning personality, large blue eyes, auburn hair and, best of all, a sweet, Christlike spirit. G—— was not a pretty girl but rather attractive and full of zeal for God. After a season of prayer, Wife approached the seekers to give what assistance she could. When she came to G—— she learned that she was having trouble over a call from God to India. She felt definitely that the Lord wanted her for the mission field, and though she had known something of it before it seemed that the Spirit was bringing her to a place of decision.

For several services she made her way to the altar to pray over the matter but failed to get help because she failed to obey the call. She was keeping company with a young man in town who was far beneath her in characer as well as in mentality and who was not a Christian. If she said "Yes" to God it would mean "No" to the young man.

I have never seen a young woman give up a young man for God but what He would send one along who was far superior. Neither have I seen a young man give up a painted doll to go with God but what He would have him a real helpmate when the proper time came.

The last night G—— was as the altar we dealt with
her as honestly and yet as kindly as we knew how.
After weeping considerably, her expression changed
suddenly; the tears stopped, she dried her eyes, and it
was quite evident that she had settled it. But how?
She arose to her feet and with jaws set, as well as
her will, and countenance hardened, she walked to
the back of the church where her friend was waiting,
and they left. It has been five or six years ago, but
I cannot forget the look on her face as she took his
arm and left the church.

She chose her own happiness but I am satisfied
she has had everything else but happiness. They
were married in a few months' time and the next summer, while passing through the town, we saw her—
not the same modest, Christian girl, but a regular
tough worldling. It hardly seems possible there
could be such a change in a person in eight months
time. But when we say "No" to God it is like tearing
down our defense and throwing ourselves open to the
powers of hell. Had G—— chosen God's will I am
sure that happiness would have been added—"Seek
first the kingdom of God and his righteousness and
all these things shall be added."

While in the West in meetings, there was a beautiful young girl at the altar seeking with all her heart.
The Christian friends were coaxing M—— to say "Yes"
to God. We learned that it was another case of God
calling and a young man standing in the way. Finally, after a great deal of desperation, she turned
her face toward heaven and told God that she was a

candidate for the mission field and that she would tell B—— that their engagement was off unless he got salvation and felt the same call. It was a beautiful sight; it is clear in my memory tonight. The all-important question had apparently been settled. With mother on one side, her friends on the other, the Everlasting Arms beneath her and the Holy Spirit overshadowing her, she was ready to take the way with God.

Without hesitation she left the altar, went out of the church to where B—— was standing and told him that was the end of their courtship. In a few minutes she returned and what a glorious illumination was upon her countenance. It was not long until B—— entered the church. His fists were doubled, his shirt pulled open at the collar, and with a scowl on his face that made us feel we were in for a trimming or, at least, a chance to see who was the best man. He came forward and with a snarl delivered a message to his father, who was pastor of the church. Then he left immediately and was gone from home for two or three days.

Without any one's knowing it, he went to see M——, promised that he would give up his sinful ways and be a Christian if she would only take him back. Taking him at his word and breaking her promise to God, she slipped away with him and they were married secretly. The next Sunday, which was the closing of the meeting, she begged him to go to the altar, but he treated her with contempt.

For about five months she lived a life of sadness,

while he, with his bulldog nature, ordered her to his own notions. With her Christian experience gone, and a husband who was as mean as the devil, she drudged along. No one knows what she suffered. At the close of five months, while in New York State, we received a telegram saying that M—— had died. We learned that she was taken sick and without becoming conscious she had slipped out to meet the living God.

We arrived in Tennessee and were greeted cordially. Faces were shining and hearts were happy. Another old-fashioned meeting was to be held, and while all hell was preparing, we were by faith calling for the artillery of Heaven.

One of the things we learned before we were there long was that L——, one of the daughters of the family with whom we were staying, was going to be married and had waited until we came to perform the ceremony. We felt very strange about it but said nothing except on our knees.

One real hot morning, with only a few in the tent for the eleven o'clock service, the Holy Ghost settled upon the meeting in an unusual way. After having preached along the line of giving ourselves to God for Him to work through, we gave the invitation, and L—— along with others found her way to the altar. God had laid His hand upon her for Christian work. What a time of praying and calling upon Him!

When we returned home she and Wife went aside and had a long talk. There was a vital question to be settled. She was expecting to be married while we were there. Her friend had rented a house and was laying in provisions for fall and winter. What should she do? God was calling, E—— was waiting for his bride. He said he loved her dearly and had even professed religion to prove it. What should she do? After service that night, L—— and Wife stood on the porch beneath the starlight canopy of heaven. L——, with tears streaming down her face, looked up and with one groan of full surrender she said, "Gladly will I toil and suffer, only let me walk with Thee." The question was settled for God's way.

The next day she gathered up all of her gifts from him and all of the letters and took them back and broke the news. How he did plead and reaffirm his love for her, but her love for God was overbalancing all human affections. We called on L—— in the meeting that night to lead the singing, and while she was giving out a number who should walk in but the young man who had so strongly affirmed his love for her in the morning, and with another girl.

Today L—— has had a Bible School training and is ready to step into the great harvest field and commence her life's work for the Master, and we can bespeak for her a life of usefulness in bringing many to the feet of Jesus.

While pastor of a certain church we had a woman in the congregation who was very prominent and appeared to be very religious. However when the doctrine of entire sanctification was presented she became very much agitated and carnality began to show itself. We understood that she was talking much behind our backs and occasionally would give us a little bit to our face, in the form of a cutting remark or a slur of some kind.

One night during Bible study class she made light of the lesson, and said some things that were a reflection on God's word. The class was dismissed and we went to our homes. Mrs. J—— and her husband retired and were both as well as usual. About half an hour after they had retired, Mrs. J—— sprang from the bed, holding her throat and gasping for breath. Her husband switched on the light and did his best to relieve her, but with little success. The doctor was called but he could not help. I went in to see her the next day and found they had propped her up in bed and were ministering to her. She continued to gasp for breath for two or three weeks. Several doctors were called but none could give the reason for it. Let us remember that some things do not have a visible, physical reason, but perhaps somewhere we have said "No" to God, or have fought His precious Word.

They later moved her to the hospital, where they tried their best to find the trouble but with no avail. Still she gasped, and with every gasp her heart became weaker. We were in to see her several times but were only allowed to stay for a few minutes, and had no chance to deal with her about her soul. Much of the time she was under the influence of morphine. She finally passed into the great beyond to face the God whose work she had fought and whom she had failed to obey. My brother, my sister, it pays to obey the Voice of God. Are you obeying Him? Will you?

CHAPTER XV

THE HOME OF THE "BEAN EATERS"

We had heard a great deal about the historic city of Boston but had never had the privilege of visiting it. Among some of the things we had heard that had stuck close to our memory were, first of all, that no one could bake beans like they baked them in Boston; another was that the folks of that city were so aristocratic and cultured that even the men on the police force had to be college graduates. I can't say that we were disappointed in the beans for they were delicious, but I hadn't been there very long when I realized that most of the police were far from being college bred men.

Well we were off to Massachusetts, a place called Medford, a suburban city of Boston. We were with a brother evangelist. He was to do the preaching and we were to take charge of the singing. With bag and baggage we landed in Medford about one o'clock in the morning. Bro. E—— was doing the driving, having been there before, while I was busy taking in the sights. Of all the parkways and boulevards, I had never seen the like before. And though Bro. E—— had been in the vicinity he became confused too. We were in Medford about three times, and in between times we were in Somerville and Cambridge, and I don't know where else. Such a Chi-

nese puzzle! I had never seen so many cities all mixed
up together, and I wondered how folks found their way
home when they went out. We finally found our
place and were given a fine comfortable room by a
good brother who had been expecting us.

In a couple of days we had our tent pitched and
the meeting began under the direction of a certain
church there. After a few days' preaching, the congregation grew and conviction settled upon the people.
Another group that seemed to grow also, both in size
and numbers, were mosquitoes. They talk about the
kind we have in New Jersey, but I never felt such as
attacked us during that meeting. However, we came
through alive with perhaps a little less blood in our
veins.

The preaching was along a straightforward line
and meant much to the Christians, since they were in
the majority. They received it with open hearts and
seemed to enjoy walking in the light. There were a
number of seekers for both pardon and purity, and
while the people grew fat on the spiritual food that
was given out by our brother, some of the preachers
became very jealous, one brother especially, who had
close relationship with the meeting.

During the closing part of the last week, the above-
mentioned preacher became so stirred that he would
visit his people during the day and try to convince
them that the preaching was erroneous, while at night
from the pulpit he would endorse the same and thank
God for such men. While the conflict raged I stuck

to my guns, sang, shouted, prayed and watched the storm rage.

We were to close on Sunday and go to another point in Massachusetts the first of the week and there have a two weeks' tent meeting. With so much feeling on the part of the preachers and perhaps some influence on their superior, the second meeting was canceled on Saturday. Naturally, we felt that wires had been pulled and plans made underhandedly.

On Saturday evening the meeting was tense, and while our brother was preaching on the conditions of the last days and how brother would deceive brother and secretly plan. one against the other, the preacher of whom I spoke, Bro. X——, jumped to his feet and rebuked him for what he had said, stating that what he had inferred was not so at all. Bro. E—— said nothing but with a very composed attitude continued his message. In a few minutes Bro. X—— jumped up again and began to abuse the evangelist. With this Bro. E—— opened fire and told him publicly what he had been doing, things that we knew to be facts. The service was dismissed but the end was not yet.

Groups stood here and there discussing the situation, while Bro. X—— was trying to get some of the folks to side with him. After a while, seeing what a show he had made of himself, he left the tent and went home. He had gone but a few minutes when the saints began to gather around the altar, one by one they dropped to their knees, and a hallowed peace settled upon them like a calm after a great storm. The Holy Ghost came with showers of heavenly blessing until, as one person, we wept and praised God for the joy of the Lord was upon us. Surely God witnessed to our souls.

At the afternoon service on Sunday many of the preachers were present, but Bro. E——, under the anointing of the Spirit, made no reference to the affair of the night before nor uttered one cutting remark, but preached the Word of God with power. In the evening the tent was literally packed, and above all God was with us. When the altar was open, they lined it and the front seats. Almost instantly victory came and the seekers began praying through until a half dozen or more were on their feet at once. The slain of the Lord were many, while others shouted, sang and walked the aisles. One dear sister danced for joy under the power of the Spirit. With all the joy that was filling the hearts of the blessed, old carnal hearts were stirred. Bro. X—— declared that the evangelist had put a spell on some of the seekers. The devil was doing his part on the outside likewise. Some one squirted acid on the tent, others threw missiles, while a crowd hooted and ridiculed. Well, glory to God, when victory comes we can expect opposition from the pit and from any one who has its essence in his heart.

Our next meeting having been canceled, we had three weeks on our hands with no work. Bro. E—— having had Boston on his heart for some time, decided that it was an open door. After some hunting we found a large hall in an old church building and were able to rent it, though at a large figure. The building was owned by a Jew and rented out for all occasions. I dare say that that was the first time he had rented it for a Holiness meeting.

We surely had plenty of people to draw from since Boston has a population of nearly a million, and there is no other full Gospel work in the city proper. Certainly a city of such size could stand a dozen churches that taught the Truth as John Wesley did.

We advertised some and opened for business. Bro. E—— was at his best and God used him mightily. At the close of the first week we were having a large attendance, while the second and third Sunday we used the main auditorium and had it about full. There was hardly a barren service during the meeting and the presence of God was manifested in a remarkable way.

A man was passing by one night and felt some unseen power drawing him in; he tried to resist but could not. When the altar call was made he fell on his face, and after getting help he stood to his feet and asked if the evangelist had something in his possession that had affected him thus. The power of God was so real that he had been literally swept into the service. The closing Sunday evening service was the most gracious sight I had ever witnessed up to that time. A powerful message was preached on the Second Coming, with perhaps forty souls at the altar (I cannot be sure about the number), about six or eight of these were children. When God began to answer the prayers of the penitents, there were about a dozen struck as though dead, while others lifted the meeting through with travail of soul. Among some of the most marked cases of prostration and soul burden were children not more than twelve years of age. It actually seemed like holy ground. Surely such scenes are seldom witnessed today.

Seeing that God had placed his seal upon the work in such a remarkable way, the people seemed to think it should continue. Bro. E——could not stay. I was planning on traveling with him that summer and there was no one else we knew of to take the work. In spite of the fact that I wanted to travel, God called me very definitely to settle down in that great city and pastor the new work. We gladly laid aside our plans, embraced the will of God and settled ourselves to another pastorate.

We commenced our regular services in the same building, with the tide running high and five meetings a week. We did not find the Bostonians of an uppish disposition, but just about like people are in other sections of the country. Our congregations ranged from fifty to one hundred and fifty, and represented several denominations. I must say that I cannot see a bit of difference between Baptists, Methodists or Episcopalians when their hearts are filled with the Holy Ghost. Surely His presence makes us of "like precious faith."

During the ten years of my ministry I have not seen such a loyal, consecrated band of saints as those that made up that congregation. Neither have I seen such displays of God's power as were manifested in those meetings. It is impossible for us to estimate the number that prayed through, but for eighteen months it was like one continuous revival meeting with but few barren services.

The children's prayer band was the greatest thing of its kind we have witnessed. About fifteen or more children, from eight to thirteen years of age, would meet in the prayer room on Sunday night about a half hour before preaching service. Such praying as they would do, many times under soul burden, many times prostrated by the Holy Ghost. We have seen them pray until the older folks sitting in the main auditorium would become so affected by it they would fall on their knees and weep and call on God. Many nights the presence of the Lord of Hosts would be so great because of the prayers of the children that it was impossible for us to go on with the regular service. Occasionally they came into the meeting from prayer and like spiritual giants swept the place with a storm of testimonies until sinners found their way to an altar of prayer. Whenever any of their number would become cold and indifferent they would round them up and off to the prayer room for knee drill. How those dear children would pray over the little backslider and weep between the porch and the altar until the lost sheep was found. My soul groans within me to see such times repeated.

Some say the young people and children must have worldly amusement and diversion, but I'm satisfied that God in His fullness can satisfy the heart of the young as well as the old. The group of children of which I have just written would rather by far have attended a prayer meeting than a party. The service of God was their joy, their pastime, their recreation, in fact their meat and drink.

We recall many of the services that took place during our stay there, and surely the memory of them is a feast to our soul. Meeting after meeting the spiritual tide would rise so high that it would seem as though the entire congregation would be translated. We have seen clearly the waves of glory sweep over the congregation like heat waves from a red-hot stove. Surely He is "the living God that changeth not."

I feel that I should speak of one service that has made a vivid impression upon my mind. It was a week-night service; there were perhaps sixty or more present and the atmosphere was as clear as could be. The Lord had laid a message on my heart concerning the faithfulness of the Holy Ghost, and I do not think we ever had more liberty or felt a heavier anointing than that night. While bringing one truth after another, we noticed that the congregation, almost as a whole, were gripped by the Spirit and sitting on the edge of their seats. When we were almost two-thirds finished, the glory struck a certain brother and with a shout he jumped to his feet and began to exhort, taking up where we left off. For at least ten minutes he lifted us into the heavenlies with words that seemed like hot coals of fire from God's altar. While he exhorted we stood by and listened, for it was as though the anointing had been taken from us and dropped upon him. When he finished, like a flash the same unction dropped in our own soul and we were able to take up the line of thought and proceed. During

the course of the message a little, timid girl of sixteen was fairly lifted out of her seat into the air like a
rubber ball. She said afterwards that she was not
aware of the fact that she sprang from her seat.

As we closed the message with the thought of the
Holy Ghost conducting us safely the last mile of the
way, the joy of the Lord was so intense, the power of
God so real and the crying and shouting so great that
we were unable to bring the message to a close. However the whole service was under the direction of the
Spirit, and, like being swept before the surging tor-
rents of Niagara, people were fairly swept to the altar
until the front of the hall was filled, benches, chairs,
floor, everything being used as an altar. Praise God
for such scenes! Would to God the church everywhere
could be in such harmony as for God to manifest
Himself in such power. Before the close of the meeting, after many had prayed through, the stately
steppings of the Son of God were so obvious that a
holy hush settled upon all and we feared to speak
aloud. At this service God was greatly magnified

At another service some months later, several were
so intoxicated with the Spirit that they staggered
like drunken men. One man was so lifted out of himself that his folks feared to have him drive them home.
When he found it necessary to stop for gas they found
him putting the ruler in the trunk on the rear instead
of the gas tank. These experiences are unusual in the
church today, but correspond to the writings of the
fathers of Methodism concerning the work of the
Spirit. When we consider the lives of those who were

thus overcome by the power of God we cannot, we dare not, question. Prostrations were common in the meetings, many times the altar service would take place before the preaching and many times there could be no preaching at all. On several occasions while we were preaching, sinners as well as saints would be knocked from their chairs and after a while would arise praising God for victory.

It is impossible for us to relate all that took place while in Boston; many things would not be proper for us to record, while there are others that we do not recall. We do know that God moved in a remarkable way through that band of saints. Immorality was uncovered, homes were made better, husbands and wives were brought together, murder cases were revealed, numbers were saved and sanctified while the church was built up in the most holy faith.

Surely it would be wonderful if such work could go on unhindered, but Hell and its forces become stirred at such victory and the result is that all of its artillery is centered on such a consecrated band.

During the beginning of the work, for perhaps the first six months, we had many things to contend with on the outside, that is to say, the devil was busy stirring up great feeling against us. Several denominations and many ministers spoke openly against us, while others that called themselves Holiness people branded the meetings as wildfire and fanaticism. One preacher said openly he would rather hear a horse thief preach than to come to our meetings. Many came out of curiosity, while others came with hungry hearts. Such opposition, such persecution, only kept us on our knees, and God, praise His name, did the rest.

We have learned, too, that where the blessing of the Lord is there is not only liberty but a desire to give. The first year the books showed thirty-six hundred dollars paid out for all purposes, and only twenty-five out of the membership were contributors. I've found in these few years that real salvation not only tenders the conscience and warms the heart but loosens the purse strings as well.

I presume the devil saw that the hotter he made it for us the more determined we were to obey the Lord, so he changed his tactics. Instead of great opposition without, he began sowing his deadly seed among the saints. Although we were more than careful as to whom we admitted to membership yet we were deceived in some and before we knew it the deadly work was commenced. The meetings would reach a high pitch and then fall flat overnight. Little by little God gave discernment, so that we were able to ferret out the trouble and finally make adjustments but not without serious harm to some and to the cause in general. With the above we can see now where we might have used better judgment in some things and thereby avoided a few of the difficulties. It is sad that God's work must be disrupted either by ignorance on our part or the carnal hearts of some professors, but these are the things that we must watch for and take advantage of the lessons that we learn by bitter experience.

Although things are not as they were with that faithful band and the work there, yet those who have pressed on are among the finest in Christendom. While they meet together, pray and sing, three of their young people are in preparation for work in the great harvest field. We take courage when we read the words of the apostle, "Our work is not in vain in the Lord."

There is one great blessing that God gave us while in Boston, that we are enjoying every day. Not a spiritual blessing but a blessing in the form of a darling baby to brighten our home.

We had been married about six years when we went to Boston. We had always loved children and hoped that some day God would see fit to send one to us, however, we had always said "Amen" to His will and were willing to go childless if He so ordered. Though the work of the Lord took the major part of our time yet there were occasions when our hearts yearned and our arms ached for a downy little bundle.

We want to take this opportunity to thank God for the chubby little baby girl that is ours. The patter of the little feet, the hearty laughter and merry chatter all make life happier and the home brighter. Though little Marjorie is just two years and three months old yet it seem as though she has always been a part of our lives.

Our chief concern is that we shall be able, by God's grace, to live before her such godly lives that by precept and example she might early see that salvation is truly the "Pearl of great price."

The prayer of our heart is that, if Jesus tarries, the little life that brings us so much joy and happiness will some day be willing to take up her cross and follow Jesus, glad to labor in the great harvest fields that she may have a few sheaves to lay at the Master's feet.

CHAPTER XVI

UNUSUAL INCIDENTS

We were holding a meeting in a certain place and for nearly two weeks we had preached earnestly but with no results. Conviction was heavy and the meetings were as tight as a drum. It was not a church revival so that we knew there were no officials standing in the way; Brother and I had rented a hall and were going at it independent of anyone, however the churches were giving us their support.

We were aware of the fact that the Spirit was leading us somewhat differently than usual, in that most all of the messages had been along the sin line, restitution and such like. We felt sure that there was some one whom God was after and endeavored to give out the truth as He directed; during the second week, Wednesday, Thursday and Friday night we were led to preach on covered sin, using different texts and going at it from a different angle.

We had held a meeting in the town about two years before in one of the churches, and had become acquainted with a number of people. Among those of our acquaintance was a young married woman who had done our laundry for us. Upon our arrival the second time we decided that we would take our soiled clothing to the same party. I went to the door with a bundle of clothes under my arm, feeling happy and face covered with smiles; I was sure that she would be glad to know that we were in town, since she had been at the altar in the last meeting. When the door was opened I spoke very courteously, told her about the meetings and then asked if she would want to do our laundry while we were there. I noticed while I was speaking that her expression was far from pleasant and when I had finished my little speech she opened fire, and of all the red-hot shrapnel from the magazine of a carnal heart, I got it right in the face. I must say when I returned to the car with the bundle of laundry I felt somewhat different than when I left. However I did have presence of mind to invite her to the services, received the final snap off and the slam of the door. I made up my mind that if she had been a convert, she must have been one of mine and not of the Lord's. I could not understand why she should act thus, since we had paid her whatever she had asked.

We noticed that the first part of the meeting she did not attend at all, later she came but sat in the rear of the hall with a very nasty scowl on her face. All of the three nights that I preached on covered sin she was there and apparently very miserable. It was Friday night, things were tense and we were desperate. We had been waiting on God all day, praying and fasting, and felt that something would have to give way or we would drop in our tracks. The altar call was given and there wasn't a single response. We plead with them but with no avail. The air was actually heavy with conviction and yet no signs of a break. Finally in despair we dismissed them, but to our surprise instead of going out they started for the altar until they were kneeling two or three abreast. I don't remember a dry-eyed seeker in the group but with strong crying and tears they prayed their way through.

When the altar service was about half over, we noticed that the above-mentioned woman was sitting back in the hall greatly moved. One of the preachers from the town was directing an invitation hymn for the benefit of those who had not made a start, when this woman jumped to her feet and fairly ran down the aisle and fell at the altar. She had not been on her knees more than five minutes when she arose, called to Bro. W—— to stop the singing, faced the congregation and with broken voice and flowing tears said that she had something to confess to the town people. There was a silence came over all while she sobbed out her story.

It seemed as though three years before, her husband had left her with two children and an infant. Realizing the struggle that she would have with an infant to care for she had killed it. No one in town had known what was the matter with the child; the doctor had given a death certificate and the thing had been well covered. Remember, reader, "Be sure your sin will find you out."

"You cannot hide from God,
   Though mountains cover you,
His eyes our secret thoughts behold,
   His mercies all our lives enfold,
He knows our purposes untold,
   You cannot hide from God.

"You cannot hide from God,
    You cannot hide from God,
Wherever you go, whatever you do,
    You cannot hide from God.
His eye is fixed on you,
    You cannot hide from God."

The town officials were there, the doctor was there, and every one was stunned at such a confession. When she had finished confessing she dropped on her knees again and in a very little while was enjoying precious Blood-bought victory.

The meetings were to close on Sunday, but with such a break we decided to stay until the next Wednesday. From Friday until Wednesday God gave us between ninety and a hundred souls. We praise Him for such victories.

We were in a certain place trying to establish a work; we had a man with us who was a great help and one that we had utmost confidence in. We had been away for some time and upon our return felt that something was undermining the cause of God in that place. There seemed to be a peculiar undercurrent that we could not fathom. Two or three weeks after our return, wife had a dream which was as follows: she saw the church building very plainly with the congregation seated, and around the outside of the auditorium was a huge snake; it seemed as though slowly it was closing in around the people and they were not aware of it. Wife and I got busy and stirred the people up sufficiently so that some of them helped us drive the snake out after a great deal of effort. Apparently everything was all right, and in the dream everything was going well when we began to notice that there were a lot of little snakes darting under the seats, etc. Wife said we labored hard to get all of the little ones out but were not altogether successful.

When she told the dream to me, immediately the Lord showed me the interpretation of it. Mr. L——, the man mentioned above, was the snake and had sowed seed among the members. Just as was portrayed in the dream, we had a job to get him out and when we succeeded found that a number had imbibed the same snake nature from him and were continually stirring up trouble among the membership. Surely the God that gave dreams and interpretations in Daniel's time is just the same today.

We were pastor in a certain city and had among our number some very godly people. We also had some that professed godliness but were, as we found out later, not in possession. One man in particular, a Mr. R——; he and his wife came into the meetings and took a great interest in them, giving quite largely of their means and professing a high state of grace. They had attended about two months when they decided they would like to join. We had been very particular about whom we had taken in as members, and were in the habit of giving them all a good grilling as to their personal experience before we would admit them. In spite of this some goats got in. We took Mr. R—— and his wife before the committee and decided that they were eligible for membership. They came regularly, testified, prayed and gave liberally.

We were having special meetings about three months later and things were tied like a knot. We were satisfied that we were up against something out of the ordinary, so went home after a meeting of the membership to pray and fast and wait upon God for direction. The same night a Mrs. M——, who was a saintly character, had retired, and while musing over the situation, the Spirit gave her a vision of Mr. R—— as being implicated in a murder. She was so pressed over it that she could hardly bear up under the awful pressure. It had not been long since the Lord had revealed to her a case of immorality and now a murder. She felt that if she brought it to our attention perhaps we would think her visionary and would not put much confidence in it. She prayed earnestly that if it was of God He would reveal the same thing to some one else. About the same time a Mrs. T—— was retiring and the Spirit showed her the same thing about Mr. R——. The strange thing about it was that neither of these women knew anything about Mr. R—— and had no occasion to find out a thing concerning his life, since he lived in an outlying section of the city and was seen only at the meetings.

The next morning Mrs. T——, not being a mature Christian, was so beside herself that she felt she would have to call some one. It all seemed providentially arranged; whom should she call but Mrs. M——, a thing she very seldom did. She told her she knew what was the trouble with the meetings and that God had showed her some things. Mrs. M—— asked whom it was about, and when told that it concerned Mr. R.—— she decided that they had better talk together. Mrs. M—— went to see Mrs. T—— and upon comparing the two experiences found that they coincided perfectly. We were notified, had an interview with them and then with Mr. R——, only to find that he was the most miserable man that we have ever seen, but not willing to confess his state. We put him through the third degree and found every evidence of guilt. We learned later that his second wife had been nurse to his first wife and that he had married the nurse just a few months after the death of the first one. We learned, too, that his first wife's people had always felt there was something mysterious about her death and had practically nothing to do with Mr. R—— after his marriage to the young nurse. Praise God! He alone can bring the hidden things to light.

"You cannot hide from God"

CHAPTER XVII

ANSWERS TO PRAYER

Truly Tennyson was right when he said, "More things are wrought by prayer than this world dreams of." Much praying means much victory, little praying means little or no victory. The man who prays much is the man who becomes intimately acquainted with God; to be on intimate terms with Divinity means to have access to His ear, to have access to His ear is to move His heart, to move His heart is to move His mighty arm that moves the world.

Abraham had such prestige with God because of his faithful obedient life that God sent him word before He destroyed Sodom, thus giving him a chance to plead the cause of his beloved nephew Lot. If there were more Christians who knew how to pray as Abraham prayed, there would be few Lots perishing in the Sodom of Worldliness, and buried beneath the debris of sinful desires.

Let us arise, Christian people, and lay hold of the horns of the altar and let the incense of prayer cause the atmosphere to be made fragrant, then will our sinful loved ones be converted, believers sanctified, the church edified, the sick healed, demons cast out, and God glorified.

In this closing chapter we will record several answers to prayer, not because we have been the ones who have prayed, for God has His praying children everywhere who are having even greater answers than these, but merely that our Lord should have the glory and some one's faith be encouraged.

After closing a series of meetings in a certain city we found that wife's lungs were affected. After taking her to several doctors for examination, and each confirming it, we were determined to do our best to see her cured as soon as possible. This was surely a blow to us and being unprepared for such news we hardly knew what to do first. We had always heard that if taken in time the disease could be cured. We immediately made arrangements for her to go to a near-by sanatarium and stay until she was well. The doctor said that perhaps two months' rest would be sufficient. We got the necessary equipment and took her to Lakeland while my brother and I prepared to go to West Virginia for a meeting.

While I was away, my folks visited her quite often and endeavored to keep her encouraged. It was a good place for her until she got rested some and the novelty wore off; during the first two weeks she gained quite a little. Then the place began to seem like a prison, the food turned her stomach and the ungodly environment began to wear upon her; being under the peculiar pressure of the disease along with all of the other unpleasant things she began to decline.

One day while father and mother were visiting her they noticed that she was terribly depressed and when they approached her about it she broke into tears. They readily saw her condition, and father went to

the office, and asked for her release. Doctor C——
plainly told her that she was welcome to go but if
she did not spend twenty hours out of twenty-four
in bed, and that for a year, it would only be a short
while when she would be gone. She agreed to do this
and the release was granted.

When I returned I found wife at home, to my surprise. She was following out her regular routine and
seemed to be bright and cheerful. The next week we
decided that it would be of great benefit to her to go
to the Catskills for awhile, so we got ourselves ready
and went to visit a friend at F——, N. Y.

It all seemed providential leading for Brother
K—— was holding a meeting about five miles from
there. Wife followed out her rules while my brother
and I attended meetings every night.

It was Sunday, and we had been at F—— about
ten days. Wife had not been out of the house except
to sit on the porch in the clear, crisp mountain air.
Perhaps you know it would be quite difficult for one
to stay home from revival meetings, who had been in
the habit of going nearly every night in the year.
Wife begged all day to go to the service that night,
but I felt that she should keep her schedule regardless
of her desires. I finally began to feel that it was
something more than desire. With this pressing upon
me I decided it was God leading.

The service was tight that evening; it was quite a
large Methodist Church and about filled to its capacity
with hungry hearts, but the official board was divided
as to the meetings. After the evangelist had labored

faithfully and not a soul had stirred, he announced that he would be glad to have the praying people stay for prayer. The benediction was pronounced and the congregation passed out, with the exception of about twenty-five who remained to pray.

We got on our knees around the altar and several prayed; the pressure began to lift and the presence of God was keenly felt; while we were kneeling, the Spirit spoke to me as to getting the saints to pray for wife's healing. I whispered to her and she was willing that they should. I got Bro. K's—— attention and told him how we felt; some oil was secured and he anointed her in the name of the Lord. While the Christians held on in prayer the Holy Ghost like lightning quickened her mortal body, going through it like a charge of electricity from the crown of her head to the soles of her feet. Before we knew what she was experiencing, our own souls were lifted until it seemed we had been translated into the heavenlies. The glory of the Lord filled the place while we shouted and praised God. I cannot explain the blessedness of that scene. Surely God touched her lungs with healing virtue.

Remember, my friend, that God never gives a single victory but what the devil will do his best to rob us of what the Lord has given. Wife was satisfied that she had been healed, yet the next day her lungs pained her worse than they ever had before. Remember, the devil can counterfeit symptoms. In spite of the pain she stood on God's promises and pointed back to the night before. When the devil saw that she was willing to trust, feeling or no feeling, he decided to pack his things and leave. Faith in God had defeated the subtle old serpent. A few weeks later she was examined by our family physician and pronounced well. Since then X-rays have revealed that there is not even a scar on the lungs where the abrasions were. Praise God, when He heals He does a complete job. "Jesus Christ (is) the same yesterday, today and forever."

One beautiful summer morning about five o'clock, with the old Model T Ford well loaded, we started for the south to hold a tent meeting. Our cargo consisted of two young men, one a singer and the other a preacher, wife and myself with about as many suitcases.

We sped along through the Shennandoah Valley; singing and praising God. Though our financial status was very low as usual, we were rejoicing in the fact that we were children of the Heavenly King. We had made the trip before and had quite an idea how much it would cost; this was enough to discourage us had we not been trusting in the One who had never failed us. The fact that we were standing upon His promise was enough to give us courage to go on. It was our first day on the road and though we were trusting the Lord to provide our needs, yet we were as economical as we could be in our expenditures.

We reached Roanoke, Va., about eleven o'clock at night and decided that we would drive along outside of the city and perhaps we could find a tourists' lodge that would accommodate us reasonably. We left the bright lights of the city and started hunting for a place to stay. We must have driven for at least fifteen miles but found no stopping place. We were all so weary that we could hardly sit up, having driven over four hundred miles that day. At last when we were about to give up in despair we noticed a place ahead; it looked nice and clean so we drove in and proceeded to inquire. A gruff voice answered us from a window above and let us know in short order that their prices were two dollars per person. We quickly decided and drove on. We had been praying earnestly that God would lead us and when we learned of the exorbitant price for a night's lodging our hearts sank and I am not so sure but what our faith went down a little, too.

We drove on and on for perhaps another ten miles or more; in our tired condition it seemed like more. There was not a tourist place to be seen anywhere and no towns through which we passed that showed any signs of life. Driving along on a very dark road, with every one in the car half asleep, we heard a report from "Lizzy"—she was out of gas. Well I was the driver and I held the purse and of course I was to blame for letting such a thing happen. I am sure the rest felt so, though they said very little. I stepped out of the car and told them I would walk to the nearest station and get some gas. I did not know whether it was one mile or twenty. About the time I was ready to strike out on foot an old rattletrap of a Ford came along with a load of colored people as its passengers. They inquired as to our trouble, invited me to climb on the running board and took me to the nearest gas station about three miles down the road. The station was closed but they assured me if I would go to the house across the road that the owner would get up and sell me some gas.

When the car drove on, there I stood on the road in a strange country about one-thirty in the morning. When I approached the yard, opened the gate and got about halfway to the house an angry dog began to bark and snarl and it seemed as if the next minute he would have me by the pants-leg; much to my surprise as well as my comfort he was tied and could only go to the end of his rope. I breathed a sigh of relief and went to the door, rapped, and in a few minutes had a hospitable Virginian ready to minister to my needs. While he was pumping the gas in my can who should drive up but the folks; some one had stopped and given them enough gas to get to the station.

After we had made our purchase we inquired for a place to lodge; the good brother informed us that the second village down the road had a nice lodging place and that it was kept by a widow. Thinking very little about the woman that kept it, but a great deal about a place to lay our tired bodies, we drove on and in a short while were learning from her that we could lodge there for a dollar apiece. That sounded more like our price, but we did not see how we would make ends met if we expended four dollars for a night's rest. We talked it over and by mutual agreement we decided that we would accept and endeavor to raise our faith to meet the emergency.

It was not many minutes until we were in our rooms and preparing for bed. Wife and I had just finished discussing the money question when she looked up and saw a motto on the wall, "Your Heavenly Father knoweth what things you have need of." Praise God, that was like an oasis in a desert land. Our feeble faith shot up like a flash, and after a word of prayer we rolled into bed feeling as if we had not a care in the world.

In the morning we were awakened by a gentle rap. We prepared ourselves and went down to breakfast. We were ushered into the dining room and introduced to a typical southern breakfast; let me say that we wasted no time in making an end of that delicious food. During the course of the meal the woman of the house came in and talked quite freely with us. It was not long until she began to tell us that she had been attending a meeting, not far away, held by Dr. H. C. Morrison. Immediately we felt at home and one of the boys who had attended Asbury College mentioned the fact. By the time we had finished our meal we felt as though we had known the dear sister all our lives. She inquired what our mission was and where we were going, etc. When we arose from the table she asked if we would go to the front room and have prayer with them; she proceeded to call in the help from the kitchen and we had a gracious time. We sang, read the Word and had prayer, and while the folks prepared to leave I prepared to pay the bill. The kind sister smiled and said when her husband died a few years before she had quite a time deciding what to do for a living. When she settled on keeping tourists she said that she promised the Lord she would never charge any of the Lord's servants. She proceeded to say that what we had enjoyed was her gift as unto the Lord. Well, Amen! We could not understand the running out of gas, etc., but God had a plan in it all and not only did our Heavenly Father know what we needed, but supplied that need according to promise.

We went on our way rejoicing, and arrived at our destination ready for action.

A few years ago while living at home with my folks we had a most wonderful answer to prayer. My brother was taken sick one Sunday and was compelled to take to his bed. He had not been well for a long time, having suffered with asthma for nearly a year. But this sickness was unusual and did not seem like the attacks that he had been having. A friend of ours, a nurse, was spending the week-end at our home and she immediately recognized that he was seriously ill, advising that we call a doctor. The doctor diagnosed the case as pneumonia and left word what should be done. Miss W——, the nurse, was engaged and began at once to minister to his needs.

When the physician came on Monday he found Brother Wesley in a serious condition and the disease only about twenty-four hours' old; he advised immediately that we had better call a specialist from Philadelphia and have a consultation. The hour was set for seven-thirty in the evening and at that time both the doctor and the specialist came. After examining Wesley very carefully they went into an adjoining room and talked for quite a while. When they were finished they came downstairs where we were standing. The specialist from Philadelphia called us into the living room and when we were seated, said to father: "I suppose you want to know the worst con- concerning your son's condition." Father replied that it was for that reason that we had called him in, and we were prepared to know the worst. The doctor proceeded to tell us the truth, stating that Wesley was very sick, his temperature was over a hundred and four, one lung was completely filled and the other rapidly filling and the disease little better than a day old; he stated that the course of pneumonia was from five to seven days before the crisis was reached, and that in view of the fact that his body was so run down from previous illness he feared that he would not be able to live to see the crisis, say nothing of pulling through it. "I'm sorry to have to tell you that, Mr. Bradley, but I want to be frank with you," he continued. It was not long until they were gone and we as a family were left alone to face the situation.

We had realized the seriousness of the situation before the consultation and had been much in prayer. To our surprise we did not feel much alarmed when we learned what the doctor thought. It seemed as though the Lord had been preparing us for the emergency and in spite of what he had said we all felt that he would get well. Several of us went to our rooms for prayer and were so assured by the Spirit that we had been heard that we came forth with our faith running high. Just before time to retire we gathered around Wesley's bed; he did not move for some time and seemed to be semi-conscious, then he rolled over, opened his eyes and looked up at me and said, "Floyd, do you think I will get well?" I told him that we felt God was hearing prayer and that I believed he would recover. His face lighted up, the tears came to his eyes and he breathed out an "Amen", turned over and went to sleep like a baby.

Immediately upon the assertion of our faith the powers of darkness assailed us and it seemed as though every vestige of hope was snatched from us in a few seconds of time. We left the room one by one and in a little while all were preparing for bed. I did not feel that I could retire until the clouds of doubt and darkness had been separated again, and I could feel that assurance that I had been in possession of just a few minutes before. I cannot easily forget that night of wrestling with the powers of darkness. It seemed for a long while that there was nothing else to do but let go and be defeated; in spite of such suggestions from the pit I continued to bombard the bulwark of hell with earnest petitions. At last, when I was about exhausted and on the verge of despair, the clouds were lifted; the blessing of God began to fall like morning dew and with it that deep settled assurance that all was well. I do not remember what time it was but it was in the early morning. I do know however that the victory was ours, that the devil had been cheated and that God was going to spare Wesley and use him in the harvest field.

When the nurse went into the room in the morning,

she said she noticed a difference in her patient; being a Christian girl and knowing that we had been praying she began to give God the glory. When she took his temperature she found it normal and his pulse likewise. This was unusual and she called the doctor. When he came and made an examination, to his surprise he found the same thing and also that the lungs that were so congested the night before had cleared up entirely. He was amazed and said to the nurse, "What have you been doing?" She replied that we had all been praying earnestly. "Well," said he, "my medicine never brought about this change." He called the specialist immediately and made the report. The old doctor assured him that the improvement was only temporary and that he could expect a rise in temperature and the other symptoms to return. He told him also that he had better examine the lungs again; said no doubt he had made a mistake.

We all rejoiced and, regardless of the prophecy of the old doctor, his temperature did not go up and in a few days he was around again praising the Lord for answered prayer. The family physician was so surprised to think that Wesley never reached the crisis and then in a few days was able to be around, that he announced it to the doctors and nurses at the hospital. We could surely sing, "Just one touch as He passes by." He is not the "Great I Was" but the "Great I AM." Praise God, today Wesley is in Arizona enjoying good health and the presence of the Lord, praying, singing and preaching when the opportunity affords itself. For a year and a half he was covered from head to feet with a running eczema, then following that for two years he suffered almost continuously with asthma, many times gasping for breath for a whole week without a let-up day or night. Out of all these afflictions the Lord has delivered him. Amen!

There are many things that I would like to record, but time and space will not permit. We just give these few instances that your faith might be strengthened and our God glorified.

I do not feel that I can bring the book to a close without mentioning one other wonderful answer to prayer. It is a recent one and has done much in launching us out into greater experiences of trusting God, and made us to feel that we should ask largely that our joys might be full.

We mentioned in the preface that my father first made the suggestion that we put our experiences into print; after several months slipped away and we had entirely forgotten about it, the Lord began to lay it upon our heart. We commenced to write about five months ago, feeling that if we were never able to put it into book form, we could at least keep it to read over ourselves. I had never kept a diary, hence I was compelled to depend on the Lord to bring the various incidents to my remembrance. Many times while writing and feeling the help of the Lord in doing it, we would think that perhaps we would give up the idea. Then the enemy would tempt us saying that we could never raise enough money to have it published if we did complete it. With all of these thoughts and impressions, yet we felt led to write on, and we did.

We were in a series of services near Kingston, N. Y., in the month of December; we were arranging our slate for the first of the year and had in mind to go to Cumberland, Md., for the first meeting after the holidays. We wrote to the pastor giving that date, but for some reason unknown to us then, he delayed writing, and in the meantime thinking that perhaps he had changed his mind we accepted a call for a point in N. Y. State. It had not been many days after we accepted the call that we received word from Cumberland that Bro. W—— wanted us for the first of the year. It seemed like a mixed up affair and we wondered if perhaps we had been hasty in accepting the call to N. Y. for that time. Well, God works in a mysterious way His wonders to perform. Having arranged other meetings it was necessary to give Bro. W——'s people a later date, namely in February. We had planned to stay two weeks with him and had made arrangements for another meeting immediately following our work in the vicinity of Cumberland. Just a few days before we were to go to Maryland we felt constrained to cancel all of our work following Bro. W——'s meeting; it was the strangest thing I had ever felt and from a reasonable standpoint it seemed that I should not do it, knowing that many evangelists were without any work. After some prayerful consideration we decided that it was the voice of the Spirit and willingly obeyed.

We landed in Cumberland, or rather the outskirts

of the city, and in the fullness of the Blessing we were ready to take up work with the above-mentioned Bro. W——. The meeting went hard for the first two weeks and it looked as though we were defeated, but having no other field to go to, we stayed the third week and with all glory to God the meeting broke and nearly fifty souls testified to either pardon or purity. We were well satisfied that we had obeyed the leadings of the Spirit in canceling our other work, for if it had not been so we would have been obliged to leave at the end of two weeks and that in defeat; "But the end was not yet, praise the Lord!" The last Sunday Bro. W—— took us to his afternoon appointment and invited us to bring the message. We had been over with him once before and the Lord had set His seal upon the service by giving us about eight souls at the altar. We had talked some of holding a service there but nothing had been said for some time. As Bro. W—— was making his announcements the Spirit of the Lord spoke to me and I was sure that we should hold a meeting in that place. I spoke to the pastor about it and while we sang something he called the official board in conference at the rear of the church and asked their opinion as to such a series of meetings. I could see by their actions that some were not very well pleased; however there were enough to carry it and the meeting was decided upon.

We commenced meetings on Monday night with about a dozen people and on Sunday night following the church was full. The first of the second week God gave us a gracious break and by Sunday there were more than fifty penitents that had knelt at the mercy bench. I must say that I have never seen a finer class of young people who were hungry for the Bread of Life than we found in that place. At the close of the altar services it was just impossible to get the folks to go home; nearly every night we would sit around the front of the church and sing, testify and enjoy the hallowed presence of the Holy Ghost. It was surely a tonic to our soul. I am confident that out of that group of young people will come some that will labor in the harvest field, if Jesus tarries. Out of more than fifty happy seekers and finders at least thirty-five of them were young people ranging from fifteen to twenty-five years old. Again we must say that we were not sorry that we had canceled our meetings and gone out like Abraham to a country that we knew not of, but "the end was not yet, praise the Lord."

A night or two before the meeting closed I made mention that I was writing a book and solicited the prayers of the people. The next night a certain person came and handed us a check for more than half of the publication price and said that the Lord had shown her that that was His will; then she added, "When you get it from the publishers I'll give you the rest of the amount." Well, glory to God, another time we were glad that we had been willing to obey the Lord and must say that we are more determined to follow closely the leadings of the Spirit than ever before. Surely God's way is the best way, though we may not see.

Let me say, dear reader, you will not lose a thing by obeying God. Can we say with Paul, "I was not disobedient to the heavenly vision"? Do not fear to step out on the promise, He will never let you down once. "Heaven and earth shall pass away, but my Word shall never pass away."

God has made it so plain that this volume should go forth to be read by many dear folks over the country, and the prayer of our heart is that these faltering words and broken sentences shall be so blessed of God as to lead sinners to trust in Christ and the saints to live more holy lives.